My Story

A path to hope

Kate Campbell

First published in 2013 by

UWA Publishing

Crawley, Western Australia 6009

www.uwap.uwa.edu.au

Republished in 2016 by Kate Campbell.

Campbell, Kate

My story: a path to hope / Kate Campbell
ISBN 9780995365506

Cover designed by Rebecca Atkinson

I dedicate this book to my mother and father – this journey would never have been possible without them by my side.

Introduction

I've been through a lot in my twenty-five years of life but I wouldn't change a thing. Our experiences make us who we are. I've experienced dark times, but I've lived to see the light. When I was nineteen, I had a boating accident that almost claimed my life and left me with debilitating mental and physical injuries. At the time, I felt let down by friends, acquaintances, politicians and lawyers and it often felt like life in general had given up on me. It was horrendous and I wouldn't wish it upon anyone. But I believe that everything happens for a reason and I've reflected and learned and can now accept what has happened to me.

The Germans have a word for it: Vergangenheitsbewähltigung . It describes a process of dealing with a past, remedying as far as possible the wrongs committed, and then attempting to move on. It's ironic that Germany has always been my safe place . It's the place I ran to when things got too much for me in Australia . What I never realised, perhaps because of my age, naivety or just plain ignorance, was that many people in Germany are also dealing with their past. And the pain in my past is nothing in comparison to what many people in Germany have endured.

The knowledge that there is always someone in the world in a much worse situation than me continually spurs me on. And I am fortunate to have an amazing support base with very loving family and friends. This is something that's worth more than gold, irreplaceable.

Writing this book has forced me to deal with my past, to face painful and traumatic memories head-on and I can look back and be proud of what I have achieved. Of course, moving on completely won't happen overnight, but I'm determined it will happen. I hope this book releases me from my past and offers inspiration to others. We sometimes forget how inspiring and supportive some people can be. How strangers can reach out and make a difference. I remember one such lady who touched my heart through a letter:

5 June 2012 Dear Kate

I began a letter to you on Friday morning and then I watched your interview on the 7.30 Report in the evening. Kate I don't know you, Luke Woollard or John Hammond or any of the families involved.

Many people in the community are thinking about you and talking about you and Luke. You both need the ongoing love and support from your families and friends. I am disappointed that you have to endure prolonged legal battles to achieve what you are entitled to. I wish you courage and strength to persevere.

I am unable to help you financially but enclose a small gift to help with correspondence costs. Please do not write a thank you letter to me! I don't want or need thanks – save the stamp!

I wish you a speedy return to good health and success in your chosen career. I'm in my 70th year and have grey hair that my little grandsons call silver! Sincere wishes that happy memories will eventually dim this sad episode in your short life.

When you are 70 and have silver hair, I hope you will be overwhelmed by joyful memories of a life well lived.

Remain strong and courageous. May the God you believe in love you and bless you. Celebrate every birthday and may peace be with you.

Kind thoughts Maureen

Maureen.

Of course I wrote back to Maureen to thank her for her kind words. I told her that when I eventually stop dying my hair, I would let it turn silver. I still read her letter sometimes.

We can all learn from one another. I've always been a philosophical person, but I suppose my experience has given me added insights of realism and courage.

With time comes change and with change comes new beginnings and this is my new beginning. In this fresh start I will always remember that life's too short to be anything but happy and I will never stop believing in humanity, regardless, and will also trust my instincts and remain set in my beliefs:

Always treat others the way you, yourself would like to be treated.
Never be embarrassed of who you are or what you've experienced.
Life is a privilege, not a right – never take anything for granted.
I could never have got to where I am today without each and every thought, prayer, letter or praise, from those close to me, from those far away and from those I've never even met. You have all given me strength and hope.

Thank You.

The Campbell clan

I grew up in the outer suburbs of Perth with my parents and my older sister. My family loved to take long road trips into the country and go camping on the weekends, all the while listening to AM radio. I loved being in the country, smelling the fresh air, hearing the sounds of nature, getting my hands dirty. It must be in the blood. My mum was a farm girl who grew up raising sheep in Boddington, a small rural town about two hours from Perth. Her family had the farm for over three generations. My great grandmother, Mandurah Nanna, received it in a divorce settlement after my great grandfather ran off with another woman after the war. Everyone thought Mandurah Nanna was mad for only wanting the farm in the settlement when she could have received so much more but that unloved little cottage meant much to her.

Mum grew up in Boddington, excelling at the District High School to year 10 and then Swan Leigh boarding school. By year 12 she had won a scholarship to attend The University of Western Australia where she studied teaching in both mathematics and physical education. But she always returned to the farm when she could and it was in Boddington where she had her first kiss with Lynden Campbell, Dad.

Dad had a different upbringing to Mum. He grew up in Claremont and attended Hollywood High. As a boy Lynden played in the cemetery and exploded milk bottles with firecrackers with his mates. He was a born romantic and at fourteen, with hormones raging, women didn't stand a chance. He left high school in year 11 to take up an apprenticeship as a carpenter before working in the public service.

Mandy and Lynden tied the knot on 22 January 1982. The ceremony was small and intimate. Lynden didn't even shave for the occasion. For their honeymoon, they saved all their money and went to Europe, even though most thought it was reckless. On their return they got a mortgage on a simple four by two house in the semi- rural suburb of Wattle Grove. Mum was six months' pregnant with her first child. Many people asked her whether the child was made in Europe, but she denied this straight away with a laugh. In July 1985 Julieanne Campbell was born. Their second child took three years before she was conceived. Me.

I was a week late, born on 7 February 1988 at 7 pm. I was happy and healthy with one small problem; I was born with a hole in my heart. My heart had to be monitored closely over my first year in the hope that nature would mend it. Thankfully, that's exactly what happened.

The Campbell family was complete.

Mum quit full-time teaching and took up sewing for a baby shop in Subiaco and Dad started his own lawn-mowing business. They knew that what they were doing would not make them a lot of money, but their jobs would enable them to pay off the mortgage and for them it was more important to watch their kids growing up, rather than get rich.

Julieanne and I fought like wildfire. If we were naughty we would face the wrath of the wooden spoon. If we swore, we literally had our mouths washed out with soap. We went to Wattle Grove Primary School, just down the road. It was very community orientated with just 80 students from pre-primary to year 7. I loved it there and graduated in 2000 to attend the local high school, Lesmurdie.

I grew up as a tomboy and loved to climb trees, race bicycles down the road and drink water straight from the hose. In summer I swam for hours on end and could name every star in the night sky. In winter I played in the cow paddock down the road and picked all the lupins in the field so the cows wouldn't get stomach- aches. Little did I realise it was actually sheep that got stomach-aches from lupins but I'm sure the 'cow-lady' was grateful nonetheless.

I loved sport and tried everything from gymnastics, dance, tennis, badminton, netball, basketball, athletics, swimming, even circus tricks. This helped with my shyness in meeting new people. At the age of twelve I was chosen to play for Kalamunda Districts Netball Association. Netball was my first love and I dreamed of playing for the Perth Orioles.

I always tried to make the most of what was on offer. I fell in love with drama and entertained the idea of becoming an actress. I joined the Lesmurdie swim team, as well as the athletics squad, and took up competitive cheerleading, performing in Queensland and Sydney at the NRL Grand Final. I also became a peer supporter, was elected for student council and began many petitions and letters for issues I saw as unjust. One was to allow surfboards on buses: How were 15 year olds meant to get to the beach if they lived in the hills and their parents wouldn't take them? From that campaign the head of Transperth wrote to say they would allow surfboards on buses that drove directly to the beach. I always got a few strange looks carrying my surfboard on the Armadale line!

I completed high school in 2005 with academic honours, the Caltex all-rounder award and a tertiary entrance exam score that was good enough to get me into any course.

That was the problem. I never actually knew what I wanted to be. I'd always hoped desitny world would help me out...

University life is the life

There were good reasons to celebrate the summer of 2007–08. I'd finished my first year of university, studying commerce and communications, all the while juggling my part-time jobs at an accounting firm and at the South of Perth Yacht Club. I was also meeting old and new friends, so the year had been busy to say the least. I met my best friend Amber on enrolment day at UWA. Ironically it's the same day I met Mark. Little did I realise at the time, but these two would have a life-changing impact on my year to come.

Mark lived around the Alfred Cove area, which was a long way from Kalamunda where I still lived with my parents. He and his school friends were a whole new world to me. They'd gone to private schools, had money and one of them even had a boat. Mark sometimes reminisced about the boat trips they took over to Rottnest, or fishing trips at Exmouth, or days spent just lazing on the river. I was in awe.

At 7.15 am on 16 November 2007, Mum woke me. I'd slept in. In a panic, I raced around my room chucking on work clothes and grabbing everything I needed for the UWA tav disco later that evening. It was the end of year party where students would celebrate the end of exams and the lazy summer months ahead. The dress code was 70s. I ran through the list: make-up, costume, straightener, shoes, toothbrush.

Wearing an unironed shirt, I grabbed my bag, a coffee to go, jammed a piece of toast in my mouth and jumped into my little red Mazda. Luckily the only traffic I would have to fight would be on Welshpool Road. From there it would be pretty easy to get on to Manning Road and straight through to the office in Applecross. I hated getting onto the Canning Bridge, it was always so scary with all the cars from the freeway, but I managed to cross it with five minutes to spare. Ironically, if I'd looked left while doing so, I would've seen the pylon that would almost cost me my life some 17 hours later.

The working day went by and at five o'clock I drove straight to my best mate Amber's, stopping on the way for a bottle of Yellowglen – it was as far as my budget would stretch. Amber and I had bought matching bright pink lycra pants that finished just below the knee. We had matching 70s hippy tops with the words LOVE scribbled over them in big colourful letters.

'Can you believe it? Everyone's finally finished exams,' I said. 'Even Ned! He just texted to say they're all sitting on the foreshore having a beer.'

'Nice,' replied Amber. 'I can't wait to dance with The Boys.'

The Boys were our group of UWA mates who were mad keen dancers. A rare treat. You'd hit the dancefloor with them and the smile wouldn't leave your face. You'd spend the night dipping and twirling, jumping and spinning, laughing and singing until you were gasping for breath. It was always the thing I looked forward to most in an evening out. That or the Deep & Meaningfuls when tongues got a little looser from the booze. Amber's sister drove us from Winthrop, down the freeway and around the river to UWA. I messaged Mark to let him know we were almost there. He said he and his mates had just rocked up on their boat at Matilda Bay and that they would come get us. I couldn't remember when Mark had organised to go to the party via boat, but it had always been the plan to hang with them before the party and have a few drinks.

Mark and and his friend Adam jumped off the jetty and came up to the shore to get us.

'I don't want to get my tights wet,' I said.

'No worries, get on my shoulders and we'll take you across,' Adam said.

Amber and I skipped along the jetty and onto the boat. There were six guys including Mark and Adam. It was such a treat for Amber and me to be on board. Everyone was in good spirits after finishing exams. Well, to be fair, only two boys had finished exams at UWA. One was Mark who had finished on Tuesday and the other I'd never met, but was told he had finished his last exam that morning and had been drinking ever since. Another guy had an exam at Curtin the next week. He left soon after Amber and I arrived. The other three on board didn't go to university. Adam and the driver had apprenticeships working on boats and I was told the other guy, Luke Woollard, had dropped out of Murdoch University.

I took the bottle of champagne on board to share with Amber. We had plastic glasses to drink out of while the guys shared a goon bag. Not all of them were drinking out of it, but those who did drank the wine directly from the nozzle . The boat started up and we putted around and in between the boats at Matilda Bay before doing a quick drive at speed in the open water.

We went past a big cruise boat of people enjoying a Friday afternoon on the water. We waved to them and a few people waved back. After no longer than half an hour we drove back into Matilda Bay and parked the boat on the sand. I was happy I didn't have to wade in from the jetty and get my tights wet.

At 7 pm the gates to the party opened and we were slowly let in to the tav disco. Mark and his friends had pre-purchased their tickets so they stayed down on the foreshore. A few people from our group went up to the bar to get some jugs of beer, while the rest of us stood outside chatting and catching up. I was having such a great time catching up with my friend, Ned, and everyone else that it wasn't until much later that I realised I hadn't seen Mark or his friends since leaving the foreshore.

I remember around 10 pm Amber accidentally tip- ped her beer over me when someone bumped her. I retaliated by doing the same, not realising hers was an accident. She told me off and I bought her another drink to apologise. Then I stopped drinking. I had acted out of character and wanted to be in control. I was also starting to get upset that I hadn't seen Mark once. I had assumed he'd make more of an effort with my friends, like I had with his.

Eventually I bumped into Adam who went to find Mark for me. We sat outside on a bench and I asked him why he hadn't even bothered hanging with my friends once. His eyes were a bit glassy. He apologised, but I wasn't convinced. I asked him whether he'd make the same amount of effort the next morning. It would be the first time he would meet my parents. I wanted him to make a good impression.

When I told Amber about it she suggested I go home with her and her boyfriend who was picking her up early, rather than go back to Mark's. But I didn't want to leave the party early and I certainly didn't want to be a third wheel. To lift my spirits I hit the dancefloor with Ned and The Boys.

As the tav closed and we were all ushered out towards Oak Lawn, everyone stood around in wild outfits talking and buzzing from the good night. A party bus had been organised to take people on to Club Bayview in Claremont. Ned knew I was a bit upset and tried to convince me to go on the bus with him.

'Come ooonnnn, Katie. We can continue to dance the night away and you can just crash at mine!'

'No thanks, Ned. Mark's meant to be meeting my parents tomorrow and it'd be too hard to get my car from Amber's in the morning and drive to his. It's just easier if I crash at his place.'

He pulled a sad face and then gave me a big bear hug that squeezed the air out of me. I watched him jump on the party bus with friends and drive away with lights and music pumping.

Adam came wandering up and asked if I was coming with them. 'I'm not too sure if I'm keen to go back to Mark's ... I don't think we worked anything out,' I said.

Adam said something along the lines of wishing Mark and I could resolve things as, even though he'd only met me a couple of times, he thought I was a great girl. He agreed that Mark should have made more of an effort with my friends, but I shouldn't let that stand between us. We walked from Oak Lawn, down the stairs and across the car park towards where the boat was moored on the bank. 'You know, Kate, you don't have to come with us if you're not comfortable.'

'I know, but it's just easier this way. Plus I have no other way home.'

'You could catch a taxi?' 'Nah, they're too expensive.' 'Here,'

he said pulling a fifty dollar note from his pocket. 'I'll pay for it if you want?'

I shook my head. Fifty dollars was the equivalent of three hours' work for me and I barely knew Adam so it didn't feel right. Besides, I was never going to stand on the dark road by myself to catch a taxi home alone from Nedlands to Kalamunda. That was a good 45-minute drive at best, and Mum had drilled into me not to catch a taxi home by myself. The Claremont Serial Killer murders were never solved after all!

I can't remember who got to the water first, or whether I was on board when the boat was pushed out. Many memories from this point became blurred. I know Adam put me in the passenger seat and then he stood behind the wheel. The only other people I knew or recognised on board were Mark, who I hadn't spoken to since our discussion, and Luke, I hadn't seen since I first stepped off the boat earlier in the evening.

When everybody was on board Luke pushed Adam aside. 'It's my dad's boat, I'm driving.'

The boat took off pretty much instantly and Luke manouvered his way around other boats moored in the bay. Once he got out to open water he pushed the throttle to go faster. I don't know how fast he was going. All I know was I was holding on to my chair and bracing against the wind. It was cold and I hung on really tight. The only other part of the journey I remember is going past South of Perth Yacht Club. I was actually meant to be working that night. I'd called up and asked for someone to cover my shift so I could go to the tav. I know it's a dumb thought, but it raced through my head, what if they knew I cancelled to be on the boat whizzing past right now.

I called for Luke to slow down.

Apparently he slowed down as we went under Canning Bridge but the police reports later stated that he must have sped up again as he was estimated to be doing about 20 knots on collision. The speed limit at night was 8 knots. The report also stated that he hit the pylon in the opposite direction in which we were headed, indicating he was doing donuts and fishtailing. My instincts told me not to get on that boat that night, but I did. If only I had known. The last thing I remember is holding on tightly. I don't know if I was afraid. I can't remember. I didn't even see the pylon.

Those four white walls

Broken left ankle
Fractured left pelvis
Collapsed left lung
Shattered larynx
Severed epiglottis
Torn oesophagus
Fractured vertebrae
Broken mandible from joint, splintered at front Loss of 7½ teeth.

I had a one-in-a-million chance of waking up from the coma. The surgeons said that if I was lucky enough to wake up, I would most likely be a vegetable. They believed I didn't have enough oxygen going to my brain because my throat injuries were so severe.

I tried to open my eyes but everything was blurry. White. I couldn't move. I couldn't talk. I couldn't breathe – a machine was doing that for me. I'd missed ten days of my life. It was all so strange. I thought I was in Club Bayview and my mind tried to reason why it had been freshly painted. And what were my parents doing there?

I thought I was wearing my pretty purple and black squared dress, not a hospital gown. I thought my male nurse was the bartender. I couldn't understand why my body wasn't doing what it was supposed to do. I was getting so frustrated.

Mum and Dad were before me bawling their eyes out. I'm not sure if it was out of despair or joy, either way I don't think the first thing they wanted me to scribble on the doodle board they passed me was: 'What are you doing here?' It took me four tries to write the words. I think Mum thought I had woken up mentally disabled. Especially after hearing the doctors' prognosis.

My parents controlled their emotions as they explained I had been in a terrible boating accident and was in Fremantle Hospital. The date was 26 November 2007. They'd received a call from the Fremantle police at 3.30 am on Saturday 17 November 2007, and were told I was in hospital with facial injuries. I had ten and a half hours of surgery on that first day. They told me how Aunty Sue, Uncle Alan, Grandma and Grandpart and Julieanne had sat with them in hospital. Mark and Adam also went to visit them. It's not what I had planned for the first parents/boyfriend meeting.

I didn't know how to comprehend it all. I was shocked. I tried to make it sink in. I had woken up from a coma filled with nightmares into something much worse: reality.

The worst part between dreaming and reality was working out what was real. I didn't know if the horrific dreams I experienced during my coma were memories relived, or whether my brain had reconstructed the events. At first I thought the accident had happened on Rottnest Island, out of the water, and that someone floated me over to the jetty on one of the chairs that had become loose from the crash. My Aunty Sue, who is a nurse, was there and helped stabilise me on the jetty. I found it so hard to breathe and my breaths were getting shallower and shallower. When we were finally permitted to take a boat back to the mainland it was dark and I was still struggling to breath, It hurts so much.

The boat was a small dingy and only two people were allowed on with me. Aunty Sue had to come because she was taking care of me. Mum and Dad stood, looking so worried. How was I meant to choose? It's like choosing which parent you love the most. I couldn't do that. I chose my sister. Of course I had never been to Rottnest.

Of course I had never been to Rottnest.

In the next dream a boat crashed head-first into a small jetty right next to the Kwinana Freeway, almost directly opposite the South of Perth Yacht Club. I crawled upward along the sand in complete agony. I knew my teeth were gone and I felt warm blood drip from my gums, down my face and trickle down my neck. I groaned and wailed in pain. Somehow I managed to crawl to the edge of the freeway and call an ambulance. I'm still not quite sure how I did this, considering I couldn't close my mouth and was choking on my own blood. To a degree I believe this dream was a warped version of reality. Maybe that was the pain I felt when I went through the boat windscreen, maybe I did feel the warm trickle of my own blood oozing down my neck.

The last and probably most significant dream was that Mark, Adam, Luke, Amber and I had the boat crash. I had broken all my teeth, but my jaw and throat seemed okay. Rather than wait for an ambulance, we decided to catch a 'water ambulance' to hospital. I worried how my parents would react when they discovered that I'd been in an accident so I decided to get my teeth fixed on the water ambulance. I entered a room with a dentist who said she could fix up my teeth in no time. She told me to strip off and lay down on the medical bed. I felt a little uncomfortable, but I did what I was told. Two large men with broad shoulders entered the room and I felt uneasy in my thin medical underwear, lying stomach down. The men began to rub my legs. This can't be part of the medical procedure, I thought. I kept my mouth shut and closed my eyes in the hope that it was all part of getting my teeth installed. As the men went to take off my underwear I couldn't hold back any longer.

'This isn't what I wanted,' I shouted as I tried to pull a robe around me. 'I think there's been some sort of misunderstanding.'

'But isn't this what you came for?' one of the men asked. He stared at me blankly. His eyes appeared emotionless and numb.

'No,' I began to whimper, 'I just want my teeth fixed.

I just need them repaired.'

The men hurriedly left the room and the lady sat me down in a dentist chair. She appeared quite flushed and worked quickly to replace my teeth and get me the hell out of her office. She worked way too quickly for my liking. Not enough care was taken. We somehow managed to escape the ambulance boat and sped away in an old yellow ute towards the hospital. By then I could hardly breathe and sat in the back tray leaning on Mark's shoulder. I knew my time was up. A nurse wandered into the car park and found me. She brought me up to hospital.

I honestly believed that was how I got admitted. It wasn't until I moved out of ICU and into my own room that I realised just how wrong I had been.

ICU

I began to grasp just how bad my situation was. The deeply concerned faces of my ever-present parents were enough to tell me I was going to be in hospital for a long time. I wanted to go back to sleep and never wake up. I didn't want to face the reality that the girl I once was had gone. I refused to look in the mirror for fear of what would see. I was convinced my face had been smashed up to resemble an ugly, toothless, scar-faced monster, who couldn't move, couldn't walk and couldn't even talk. I was trapped.

The following days in ICU were a bit of a blur. I was heavily medicated for my pain and each minute seemed like an hour, each hour was a day. If someone asked me how long I was there for, I'd have to say it felt like the majority of my hospital stay. Really it was only about two weeks. The hardest thing was not being able to move or talk; and my body hurt so much, everywhere, that I just lay flat on my back for days.

My whole mouth was wired shut because I'd broken my jaw in several places and it had to be reconstructed and put back together. As I ran my tongue along my teeth I felt wire and my first thought was that I'd have to have braces as the lady in the dream hadn't done a good enough job. When I became more aware, I realised that the wires weren't holding my teeth in place but, rather, my teeth had been knocked out. The wire was actually holding my jaw in place and was attached to the few remaining teeth in my mouth. The tracheotomy tube in my throat was the worst. I actually tried to rip it out while I was unconscious. Luckily my nurse managed to stop me before I did too much harm, but I did do a lot of damage to the equipment. With a bit of repair work I was lucky enough not to need a new tracheotomy tube. That would have meant yet another operation. And, to be fair to the tracheotomy tube, it did save my life. I'll assume that you do not know what a tracheotomy tube is or does. So I will attempt to explain as best I know how.

Basically, my throat was so badly damaged that I couldn't swallow and any saliva , blood or mucous just pooled in my throat. I had a cuffed trachea which was pretty much a tube inserted at the base of my throat that was attached to a balloon . The balloon was inflated and acted as a stopper to catch all the liquids pooling in my throat before they got into my lungs so I wouldn't drown in my own fluids. The trachea tube had a little gadget attached that enabled me to see the pressure of the inflated balloon.

I wasn't drowning in my own fluids so that was all well and good, and I had a hole in the base of my neck so that I could breathe – but what about the liquids pooling in my throat? The answer – suctioning. The nurses put a long thin tube into the trachea tube and up to where the balloon was situated. They then suctioned out the pooled liquid every hour. At first I watched the liquid being sucked out with fascination. It was always a yellow colour with specks of red throughout. Eventually suctioning became one of my most hated aspects of hospital.

I coughed and spluttered. It was painful and uncom- fortable. It got to the point where every time I was suctioned, I would grip the edge of the bed and squeeze my eyes tightly. Small tears would always escape.

One thing that took my mind off suctioning was the endoscopies. They were unforgettable. For the first one, my ENT surgeon and his intern came in to ICU to have a look at the surgery on my throat. At this point, I was breathing on my own again but needed continual suction from my trachea tube. The tube was a lot lower than a normal trachea as the damage I had done to my larynx, oesophagus and epiglottis, well I guess the whole throat area in general, was extremely severe.

The doctors raised the top half of my bed with the controller so that I was almost sitting upright. One of the doctors held my hand and said everything was going to be okay and that it may be a little uncomfortable at first. I watched as they wheeled a big black machine over to my bedside and produced a black tube that was actually the camera. They began to moisten the camera with a lubelike substance so that it would easily slide into my nose. I didn't get any numbing spray as I couldn't swallow and the extra fluid would make my throat worse and mean more suctioning.

My left nostril was already used to having a permanent tube attached to it. The tube went directly to my stomach and dripped liquid food at a constant rate of 30 mL an hour. I closed my eyes as the intern approached with the camera cable to put up my right nostril. I squeezed the doctor's hand so hard as the staff slowly inched the tube through my nose and down into my throat. The doctor calmed me by stroking my arm and squeezing my hand ever so gently in return. It didn't stop the tears.

After the scope the doctors said they were quite pleased at how everything was looking. I found out weeks later that they really couldn't make out anything because my whole throat was covered in mucous and saliva , but I guess they didn 't want to tell me at the time. It was one of the last things I needed to hear. At that time I thought it would only be a week or two before I could finally eat again . Little did I know that food wouldn't touch my lips until many months later.

I did so much while in ICU. I don't know the time- frame I did it all in but each minor step was a major accomplishment. I remember doing 'physio' while lying flat on my back by waving my arms in the air. The biggest concern for everyone was that I would get a lung infection or pneumonia from lying still. I had a collapsed left lung and a tube coming out the side of my chest just under my left arm, draining all the fluids. I knew it would leave a reminder scar.

A few days after waking from my coma, a nurse, or he could have been a doctor, came and took that tube out. He chatted to me, but I can't for the life of me remember what he said. It's a weird feeling seeing a tube coming out from the inside of your body through a hole in your underarm. I've never been squeamish with needles, so I watched every single tube the staff took out of me, as well as every single tube or needle they put into me.

I slowly started to get feeling back in my mouth but because of the metal I couldn't grind my teeth, wiggle my jaw, nothing. My teeth were clenched together, with my teeth resting on top of one another and my tongue on the bottom of my mouth. My teeth couldn't come apart. I couldn't even lick my lips. I also couldn't brush my teeth (what was left of them anyway). It made me feel so disgusting on top of everything else. The remaining teeth I had weren't even being taken care of. I guess I wasn't eating so at least the foods wouldn't wear them away.

No matter how many times people had explained it, I still couldn't understand what had happened to me. My high-school girlfriends brought me luxurious presents, like creams and soothing lotions. They encouraged me to smell them, not realising my tracheotomy tube was the only way I could breathe and that no air would pass my nostrils to trigger my sense of smell. I still couldn't grasp the fact that one moment I was heading home from a party and the next I was in a foreign bed with tubes coming out everywhere. Spending so much time lying in that hospital bed really made me consider the value of time. How would I get back the ten days of being in the coma? And how much time ahead of me was I going to be lying between the hospital walls? How much was time worth? I'd always been someone who could never sit still. I loved to be outdoors, trying new things. I craved the sunshine and relished the waves. Summer was my calling. Even though I was going to work full time over the uni break, I had planned on spending every waking moment outside of work down at the beach.

Critically stable

The day I was scheduled to leave ICU they decided it was time to take my catheter out. I know people think catheters are horrible, but for me it was the best thing in the world. It hurt so much to move, so the fact that I never had to get up to go to the toilet was ideal. To remove the catheter, one of the nurses helped me out of bed and placed me on a chair. I don't quite know what the nurse did to take it out, but I remember the uncomfortable feeling as it was pulled through my body. This was one hospital procedure I was not prepared to watch.

I was returned to bed and then lifted up into a sheet and swung onto a mobile bed, like the giant milk- shake game you did as a kid when your friends would swing you by the arms and legs. It was similar to how they weighed me. I was admitted into ICU weighting 62 kg and two weeks later I was leaving at 58 kg. I was wheeled into my new room, which had a great view of the Fremantle harbour and the Dockers' footy oval. Mum brought in binoculars so I could check out the boys at pre-season training. She also purchased some pyjamas that were big enough to wear over my tubing. I didn't have to wear a hospital gown anymore!

The first couple of nights in 7 North Room 12 I had to have an orderly sit with me as I was still in a stable, but critical, state. On the first night, I couldn't sleep and wrote on my doodle board to the orderly, a lovely young lass who was studying at uni. The next night I had a man watch over me. We chatted away, well he did and I wrote on my doodle board telling him about my accident. He said that he had been hit on the head by a jet ski a few years ago and also suffered serious injury. He showed me the scars on the back of his head and told me it was great I was alive. I let him read through all my surfing mags while I dozed in and out of consciousness. I wish I could remember his name. It was when I was in this room that I discovered the book of letters. Mum had left a book in the ICU waiting room for friends and family to write in. Only two people were allowed to visit at any time so it gave others something to do while waiting. She also thought it would help people to feel like they were talking to me while I was in my coma. She wrote: It has helped me to jot down what is happening, though I doubt I'd ever want to remember this in years to come. I love you, Kate. Never give up; you've come so far already.

I've always believed I have a guardian angel watching over me, but knowing that I had such great friends and family really gave me the additional support and encouragement I needed. Little did I know when I first read those kind words that I would read and reread them to get through the long days in the months and years ahead.

After Mum, my friend Kath was the first to write in the book. She came to visit me on her birthday, which was so touching. After her, Mark, Adam and Amber came. I loved knowing they'd come together and had written in the book. One of my best mates Jay made me laugh with her entry: Oooohh! They are giving you a wash at the moment. You def needed it you dirty girlie! She also wrote of the time we became blood sisters and that it made our bond stronger. She talked about having an enormous gathering when I got better. Other friends told me I looked beautiful even with my tubes and sexy blue and white striped hospital gown. They told me how much they loved and missed me.

Amber came to visit every day and told me she got phone calls from at least five people from uni daily and added, your hair looks great at the moment, and I have to say I find your nighty rather sexual (mainly coz I'm presuming it shows your bum!). Some friends had taken up swimming at Fremantle pool so they could exercise after visiting me. I even got a paw print from my dog, Abi.

My cousin, Bec, wrote:

I have looked up to you my whole life Kate, you're so beautiful, so smart, so caring and so loved. You have made us all so proud and I know you will keep making us proud coz you're gonna get better, I know you are.

Reading Ned's typed and pasted note, though, really made me think about how life might have taken a different turn. It made me understand how important it is to trust your instinct. To understand that while you yourself might be a responsible person, you can't assume everyone is. If only I had gone with Ned that night.

Hi Kate!

I decided to write you here coz I can't talk to you any other way! All I want is to come in to your room right now and jump into your dreams and say hi and tell you that everything is going to be okay. You truly are an amazing super special awesome person. If you even think of giving up I will die myself, really, not an option missy so don't even think about it!

It feels weird typing this, knowing that you aren't going to read it until you're awake. But at the same time, it's also a prayer for you now. You are always in my thoughts and in my prayers. Mum was at church the day after the accident happened and prayed for you in the segment where the priest says a prayer for everyone. Basically anyone in the church may say out loud someone they are praying for for everyone else to hear, you had the whole church of prayers going for you! Hehe I'm blabbing I know, but I figured through all your interesting and full on times at the hospital you've got a bit of time to read my dribble ☺

I keep re-thinking the night and wishing that I had brought you onto the bus with me and got your ass to Clubba! Haha it was crap anyway so you didn't miss out on much. However, you woulda been safe, with me, tucked in bed at home the whole night. I am so sorry that I wasn't there for you. I know it's not my fault and blahdie blah, but I feel like I have the need to protect you! Forever more I promise, promise to be there for you whenever you need okay? That was the case before, and I know you knew that, but still, always and forever okay?

All I want to do is see you smile again. You truly do light up the room with your eyes when you smile and it's just not fair that this has happened to you. But you're a strong girl and I know you will make it through. Amber said you'll hopefully be home in time for Christmas?! That's awesome. Yay!

I know you're still with us, I don't know how I know, but I just feel that Kate Campbell will be back with a vengeance when you recover! It's funny how things that don't kill us most definitely make us stronger. I wish I was allowed to come and see you even if you're not awake and even though you might not be able to respond,I'm sure you'll be able to hear me, and, if not, our thoughts and souls can talk to each other to our hearts' content ☺

I am writing this on my brand new laptop, sitting in bed late at night. I find it hard to sleep sometimes, and when my thoughts wander they often wander to you, wondering if you're okay … I think I'm repeating myself but I'll say it again anyway: I am always, always with you okay? If not in person then most definitely in spirit. I love you so much!

Changing the tube

The male nurse I had on the first night in Room 12 had a big chopper moustache, grown for Movember. All the other nurses on the ward were female and were greatly looking forward to it being shaved off the end of the month. There were some light moments at the hospital and at times I felt encouraged, but not knowing the full extent of my physical injuries made me really anxious. Probably the hardest thing was not knowing if I would ever be able to eat again. When I was transferred I thought, things are only going to get better from here. To a degree that was true, but on the other hand I had no idea what I was in for.

My throat surgeon had to see if I could maintain and clear liquids without the cuffed tracheotomy tube. If I could do so they would be able to change the trachea tube to a smaller trachea tube without a balloon attached inside my throat. That meant periodically deflating the balloon cuff on the tube to see how my airway reacted, a procedure known as 'de-cuffing'. I couldn't risk a lung infection on top of my collapsed lung and I was still unable to swallow so I was just spitting constantly. Any liquid that snuck down my airway would be coughed back up through my trachea tube. I practiced being de- cuffed for small periods each day. Eventually the periods became longer, until I was able to maintain it for a whole two days without needing to inflate the balloon. Only then was the surgeon confident I could maintain and clear my airways myself.

He was going to change my tracheotomy tube for something a little smaller. The hole at the base of my throat was quite large and the tube I currently had was attached to a machine that ventilated and filtered the air into my lungs. I can't even describe how scared I was. I thought I wouldn't be able to breathe or I'd choke and die. The doctors had to talk calmly with me. Dad said he would leave the room but I asked him to stay.

I gripped the edges of the bed tightly and squeezed my eyes shut hoping and praying that it would be over in just seconds. I felt the doctor pull at the stitches that held the tube in place. That hurt a lot but I knew there was more to come. When he yanked out the tube a lot of mucous and skin came with it. I couldn't breathe. I didn't have an airway. I panicked. I thought I was a goner. I don't know if you've ever had a drowning experience before, but when you realise you can't possibly get air anymore, it's terrifying. When the doctor finally inserted the new tube I gasped for breath. They told me to calm down but everything hurt so much and the world started to spin. Dad sat at the end of the bed. His eyes welled up.

To my amazement, they didn't sew the new trachea tube in. I had to hold it every time I tried to cough because there was the possibility it would just pop out. I tried my best to use the suction port as little as possible and would only ever use it if I needed it to suck up mucous, blood or saliva that I couldn't cough up. I had to learn to cough again and I was desperate to be able to clear my throat on my own without the help of the machine . Each day I got a little better but it took at least a month until I rarely needed the suctioning.

I coughed an awful lot because I couldn't swallow. I went through three to four packs of tissues a day to catch everything I coughed up out of the tube, but some of the time it was difficult to judge when coughing would start and it would just spray over my bed sheets, shirt and sometimes even the wall. It was hard sleeping and coughing at the same time. I had to make sure my hand covered the trachea in case it popped out. Sometimes I woke up not breathing at all because so much mucous had blocked the tube so I had no 'airway'. I'd press the buzzer in panic, desperate to breathe. Hoping a nurse would arrive in time.

As the weeks wore on I learnt how to clear the tube myself. This involved popping out the internal plastic tube and scrubbing it inside and out to clear the mucous away, before putting it back inside the larger tube again. This would be done every few hours. At first I was proud I had mastered the cleaning, until it slowly dawned on me that

I might need the tracheotomy for the rest of my life, going home with it and clearing it forever.

Having the tracheotomy tube in meant that I couldn't talk. I had assumed that when it would finally be taken out I would be able to talk straight away. What nobody told me was that I'd damaged my vocal chords and larynx so significantly that not only could I not speak at that moment with the trachea tube in, but it was also likely I would never talk again.

I was assigned a voice therapist and at one of my ENT endoscopes she asked me to block the trachea tube with my finger so that no air could be inhaled or exhaled. She told me to relax and try and say the letter 'A'. I tried my hardest. Nothing came out. Not one sound. Not even a gurgle. I was distraught. She encouraged me to try again and I was so determined to find my voice that I pushed every functioning muscle in my throat to produce the gurgliest, quietest 'A' sound. I was ecstatic. With daily voice exercises, I would talk again. Knowing just how well would be a matter of time.

From one tube to another

It was probably a month into my hospital stay that I began to get depressed and worried that I would never be able to eat again. At the beginning of December, a couple of weeks after I was admitted, I underwent another operation to have a PEG (percutaneous endoscopic gastrostomy) tube inserted into my stomach to replace the feeding tube that went through my nostril. I was losing weight rapidly and the doctors decided this would be a suitable long-term solution for feeding. I realised that they sought a long-term solution because of my inability to swallow. If I didn't learn to swallow, I would never eat or drink again.

Because my jaw was wired tightly shut and I had so much damage to my larynx and oesophagus they couldn't put the camera down my throat, the only option was to slice me open, find my stomach through the newly slit hole, insert the PEG tube and then sew me back up. The PEG tube went directly to my stomach through my abdominal wall and dangled outside my body. At the end of the tube was a small plug that I could pour liquid food into and it would slowly drain into my stomach. That's how I'd eat. Meal in a can! A convenient way to survive if you can't swallow. I guess it was better than starving to death.

When assessed by the nutritionist I was meant to have four to five cans of Jevity a day at 325 mL per can, but after the operation I had so many problems with the tube that I lost a good four to five days of 'eating'. Not having a nose tube attached to a machine all day enabled me to be more 'active' and get out of bed more often. The only downside was that after feeding time, which was half a can every three hours, I would feel violently ill and be unable to move for fear everything would come back up. I had the tracheotomy at the base of my throat to breathe and as Jevity came back up, not only would it come out my mouth and nose, but also out my tracheotomy tube, my one and only breathing source. Once that was blocked, I was done for.

I remember one time when my parents were visiting. I could feel the vomit rising in my throat and my stomach was whirling like the ocean on a stormy day. I forced myself to sit up as the first vomit projected out of my mouth and all over my bed. I tried to breathe, but my trachea tube was blocked with liquid. I banged my fists on my bed in desperation as I coughed and spluttered, gasping for air, but getting none. Nurses were called and my parents were rushed out of the room as a code blue was activated. Doctors and nurses quickly contained the situation and a suction tube was stuck directly down my trachea into my throat to capture any liquid before it went into my lungs. If the liquid had found its way to my lungs it could have prompted pneumonia, chest infections and possibly another operation.

My throat burned, my chest burned, my stomach ached and I continued to vomit as the suction tube jabbed at the back of my throat. After a time I was considered stable but nobody was allowed to come in my room.

The vomiting attacks continued to occur every couple of days and the doctors ended up putting me on a variety of anti-nausea drugs. No matter what cocktail of drugs I took, I lost more and more weight as the days wore on. I was becoming weaker and weaker because my body couldn't get the nutrients it needed to regenerate. I realised if I kept going this way I would starve to death.

And so this is Christmas

Christmas came to bring some cheer. It was as good as Christmas in a hospital could be. Mum, Dad, Julieanne, and her boyfriend, Daniel, wheeled two big washing baskets full of presents from the car and through the ward. The nurses thought they were doing rounds for the whole hospital but they were really only stopping in on one room.

Dad entered my room wearing a Santa suit, yelling 'ho ho ho'. Mum, Julieanne and Daniel followed closely behind wearing Christmas hats. Mum had decided that no-one could open presents until we were all together at the hospital. Julieanne was like a little kid, desperate to open hers. My jaw was still wired shut and I couldn't talk so I was allowed to choose who went first. I picked a present out for Mum and then we each took turns from there. Amber and Rob, my high-school sweetheart and good friend, had both popped a present in the basket for me too. Amber got me a white ukulele and Rob bought me a Santa shirt, which I put on immediately. Mum bought me a sushi making kit. I loved sushi but wondered if I'd be able to eat it again – I tried to hide that disappointment from Mum.

Around mid-morning my extended family arrived to join in the festivities and my room was full of people trying to put on a brave face and make the best of a bad situation. My cousin Chris was an orderly at Swan District Hospital and he decided it would be nice to take me for a burn in my wheelchair outside. It was a ridiculously hot 40-degree day, but it was so good to be outside for a change. The warmth of the sun on my skin and a trickle of sweat down my back made me feel human again. Chris and I wheeled around the car park doing broggies until Aunty Sue told him off. I was enjoying myself until everyone left to go back to Mum and Dad's for lunch. My condition was still considered too critical to go home.

Just as I began to feel lonely and sorry for myself, Jay came to visit. She brought with her a Christmas pamper package! It was full of delicious creams and face-masks and even a complimentary massage! Jay originally started her career a beautician so she set to fussing over 'making me beautiful'. She even shaved the leg that wasn't in a cast. Unfortunately she wasn't allowed to paint my nails, as patients can't have nail polish on during surgery and I was hoping to get my jaw unwired before the New Year.

A Pommy friend, Harri, and her mum turned up mid-afternoon. Their family was on the other side of the world so I think they enjoyed spreading some Christmas cheer to someone in a dire situation. It was the first time I had met Harri's mum and she was absolutely lovely. She even brought me a Christmas card.

Then Ben, my ex-boyfriend before I dated Mark, popped in. His visit came as quite a surprise as he'd only ever visited me before with a friend by his side. He brought with him a Christmas card from his parents and gave my hand a squeeze as he pulled up a chair. After a bit of chatting with my doodle board he picked up my guitar Mum had brought in and started strumming.

He sang songs of the past: from our time in high school and from when we were together. I closed my eyes and got lost in the music. Ben stayed and talked, and played and sang until visiting hours were well and truly over. He really made my Christmas; but as he sang, I realised that I missed him. As he went to leave it occurred to me that if we had still been together, none of this would have happened.

When he left the room, I burst into sobs. All the built-up emotions and the whys and what-ifs hit me with force.

If only I could have made it work romantically with Ben, then I wouldn't have got with Mark and I wouldn't have got on the boat that Luke was driving and I wouldn't be lying in hospital on Christmas Day…

I thought about Julian. I'd met him in Germany when I was there as an exchange student in 2006. He became my boyfriend. If only I'd continued with him in a long distance relationship I would never have got together with Mark and I wouldn't have got on that boat and I wouldn't be lying here.

If I had never studied German, I would never have met Mark so I would never have …

If I had chosen a different country instead of Germany during my exchange year, then I would have never studied German …

There I lay unable to eat, talk or walk. Merry fucking Christmas right? I was exhausted from the crying. I wish I could say I cried myself to sleep, but I didn't. All that ran through my head that night was, 'When will it end? Why the hell did I choose to live?'

(Un) Happy New Year

Two days after Christmas I went for my next procedure and had my jaw unwired. This was around the same time that my trachea tube was taken out. I was able to breathe again through my mouth and nose. I thought they would have sewn up the hole in my throat, but all they did was pop the tube out, put a special round bandaid over the top and that was that. I was told that whenever I coughed I had to press the hole to keep it shut. I also had to press the hole to talk, otherwise it could rip open. The hole was meant to heal naturally over the next few weeks.

Being able to move my jaw again was the strangest thing in the world. It was painful. My jaw had remained locked in the same place for six weeks. I was given exercises to practise movements again which included inserting large pop sticks between my back teeth to lever open my jaw. One pop stick at a time. When I first tried, I couldn't open my mouth wider than a finger. I made it my aim to add one pop stick every two days and, with great patience, after a week or two I was able to open my jaw wide enough to fit two fingers in.

I was beginning to feel like a new woman. I could finally brush my teeth again. I thought it would have been awesome. But it wasn't. I had one half-cracked tooth and another exposed nerve. Any air that rushed past was excruciatingly painful and if I knocked it with a toothbrush it was killer! I can't remember who came to visit during this period, all I know was that I was trying desperately hard to get myself well enough to finally go home.

I saw in the 2008 New Year lying in my hospital bed surrounded by Mum, Dad and Amber. Mum and Dad snuck in a bottle of red and pizza. I was still trying to the idea that I

might never eat or drink again. They were the first people I allowed to eat or drink around me. The smell of food was torture for me –

even the hospital meals being wheeled along the corridors tormented me. I was very malnourished and had lost a good 10 kg in hospital.

Hospital visiting hours were supposed to end at 8 pm but that didn't make my family leave and it didn't stop Ned from arriving. He and a few of The Boys had tickets to the New Year's Eve party at the Norfolk Hotel in Fremantle. Seeing as the hospital was so close, some slightly tipsy lads decided it would be a great idea to sneak in and give me an end of the year surprise.

At about 9 pm The Boys waited until someone exited and then they snuck through the open doors and up to my room. Mum, Dad and Amber were still there. We all sat around talking and laughing, while one of the guys gave me a shoulder massage and Ned and another guy discussed how to take apart all the machines in the room. That's engineers for you!

I was discharged on 4 January 2008. It took me ages to pack up my room. I had been given so many teddies, flowers and books, a German flag, and my wall was covered with pictures and posters from friends. The whole windowsill was lined with letters and cards. We made our way to the car, which Mum had parked as close to the hospital as possible. I was still very weak and on crutches. Driving back to our house, I was so excited. I was out in the world again. I wished I could stick my head out the car window like a dog and enjoy the wind blowing my hair back.

The first thing I did when I got home was give my dog a gigantic hug and from that moment she followed me around everywhere. I still couldn't talk properly and she knew that something terrible had happened so she didn't want to leave my side. Mum brought home a big box of tin cans full of liquid nutrients. It would be my food for the next month. The first day I enjoyed being home, but as I tried to settle back into life again I realised everything had changed. I had to carry a 'spit bag' with me everywhere as I was still unable to swallow. The average human being makes 1.25 litres of saliva a day. We swallow all that subconsciously. The muscles in my throat weren't working; the nerves that would ordinarily tell my throat muscles to swallow had been severed so even when I consciously tried to swallow – I couldn't. I spat 1.25 litres of saliva into a bag each and every day.

My energy levels were also extremely low. I could hardly walk from one end of the house to the other – even though it was only a distance of 15 metres. It was an exhausting walk and I'd stay seated in the lounge room all day until I made the 15-metre walk to my bedroom at night. When I slept I lay flat on my back so my PEG tube wouldn't leak. Even though the tube was corked, sometimes it would slip open and whatever stomach acids or liquids remained in my stomach would drain directly out of the tube and onto my bed and nighty.

Mum bought a special marble crusher to grind up all my tablets and pour into my PEG tube. I was still on anti-nausea medication that I had to take three times a day before feeding. Half an hour after the meds, I'd sit in front of the TV with my tube popped open with a giant syringe that poured the liquid food. Each can took about half an hour.

I always had a bucket next to me as I often vomited during this process. My stomach couldn't tolerate it and I started 'eating' less and less. After a week I was down to less than a can a day. Eventually I gave up trying to eat all together. Even water made me feel ill. I don't know whether it was the liquid hitting my stomach directly or the food itself, but I was in dire need of help.

The six-step process

My parents forced me into the car and began driving towards Fremantle Hospital. I tried to yell for them to stop the car, but it only came out as gurgle. They wouldn't stop. I threatened to throw myself out on Roe Highway. I opened the door and Dad pulled over into the emergency stopping lane. Both he and Mum were crying. They didn't know what to do.

I was dying of starvation. I knew I needed help but I didn't want to go back to hospital. I'd only just returned home. I wanted to be well again. I wanted to be normal. Eventually I gave in and crumpled into the back seat, whimpering. I knew I had to go and there was nothing I could do about it. I hadn't eaten in so long I'd forgotten what it felt like to be hungry.

Mum and Dad sat with me in the emergency room for six hours while the staff organised a room for me. By late afternoon I was finally allocated one in the same ward as before. I became really depressed. The nutrition- ist visited me and said we needed to find a solution. I told her I literally couldn't stomach that stuff anymore and suggested trying something else. I was told there was no alternative. We came to the short-term compromise of being attached to a drip for three hours on, three hours off. The food slowly dripped, millilitre by millilitre, into my stomach via my PEG tube and a drip in my arm replenished my fluids. I was extremely dehydrated.

I stayed in a hospital for about a week. I told myself to toughen up; that this was my life now and I had to deal with it. The little kid inside of me jumped up and down. It cried and chucked tantrums, but I refused to let it win. I decided I was going to eat again. I was going to be able to swallow. I was going to fight.

I set a plan:

Step 1) Start swallowing my own saliva.

I had a few endoscopies when I got readmitted to hospital and, even though nothing was certain, it seemed like the muscles in my throat had slight movement again. I was ecstatic. I started trying to swallow my saliva instead of spitting. I started using my spit bag as a measuring guide to show me how much I could reduce my spitting by.

I refused to empty the bag (gross I know but I had to see if I could swallow any) and on the first day I managed to get just below a litre of spit in to the bag. On the second I spilled the bag. On the third day I tried to swallow every single mouthful of saliva. Even if I choked on it, I'd have another go, and then another and another, until I finally got it down. Sometimes it would take fifty goes.

By the time I finally left hospital I had gained a kilogram or two and my spit bag was down to less than 250 mL. I was thrilled. My aim was to get rid of the spit bag before uni started. How embarrassing would that be? I got home just before Australia Day on 26 January 2008. My girlfriends came round for a swim in the pool but I couldn't swim with my PEG tube. I knew if I ever wanted to dive into that cold water again I had to have the tube removed. That's when step two kicked in.

Step 2) Start eating soft foods.

A speech pathologist came to our house twice a week for an hour. She was lovely and gave me lots of exercises to try – not only with speaking but also with swallowing. I was so excited when she let me try to swallow a teaspoonful of yoghurt. She said she'd give me five goes. I completely choked on the first teaspoonful. The second mouthful was just as hard and so were the remaining. I was so disappointed. I was swallowing most of my saliva by now and only spat occasionally. She said we'd have another go the following week.

In the meantime I was given exercises to strengthen my throat muscles.

I had to lie on my back, arms by my side and lift my head slowly with my neck muscles, hold, and release. I was meant to repeat that exercise ten times, three times a day to make my larynx stronger and promote movement. I placed my finger on my Adam's apple (yes, even girls have one) and swallowed to feel the larynx lift up. Mine didn't move one bit. It stayed right where it was with each attempt to swallow. From my understanding, as the larynx lifts it uses other muscles to coordinate closing the airways and opening the oesophagus so food goes into your stomach and not your lungs. I decided if my larynx wasn't going to move I was going to make it move!

Step 3) Do throat lifts thirty times, ten times a day.

Yes this step was extreme, but I wanted to make my muscles strong again, or at least make them work. I figured it was like going to the gym. The more I did the exercises the more likely my muscle would move and become strong.

The next time I tried to swallow a teaspoon of yoghurt I succeeded. By the third week I coughed and spluttered up three out of five teaspoons, but two would make their way down. I eventually got there and was then allowed to try and move on to different textures.

Mum went on a shopping spree and bought all things gooey. I got to try YoGo, rice pudding, baby food and fruit puree. Some foods were harder than others – the puree stuck to my throat, but no matter how much I choked or how many times I tried, I persisted until it went down. When no-one was looking I became adventurous and started trying things I wasn't really ready for. Mum and Dad started feeling okay about going back to work and leaving me on my own. When they were out, I tried the hardest thing of all: liquids.

People might assume that liquids are easy as they can just slide right down your throat. That was the problem. If they slid down my throat and into my lungs I was in trouble. I was very nervous and had to really concentrate to direct the liquid into my stomach. I started off with little droplets at a time. After a few days I could manage swallowing mouthfuls reasonably well. I think Mum and Dad wanted to tell me off, but I was doing so much better than expected. What were they meant to say? 'No, Kate, you are not allowed any water!'

Commercial baby food was just horrendous! Mum began to puree mashed potato and mashed vegetables to give me a bit more variety. Once she even tried to puree spaghetti bolognaise! It was pretty lumpy and hard to swallow, but it was the best meal I'd had in a long time. I still had to eat everything by the teaspoonful and concentrate really hard to make my muscles work together so I could swallow the right way. Often I'd choke, but at least I was actually eating. Mind you, I still had my stomach tube and was still being liquid-fed, but at least I was finally gaining some kilos.

I had ticked the first steps off my list.

Step 1) Start swallowing my own saliva. . ✓

Step 2) Start eating soft foods. . ✓

Step 3) Gain muscle movement in my throat. Now it was time to focus on the next ones: . ✓

Step 4) Get my PEG tube out.

Step 5) Return to uni. . ✓

Step 6) Carry on with life and appreciate it. ✓

Step six was easier said than done…

A whole new world

It was hard to deal with 2008. When I finally got out of hospital the second time, just before Australia Day, I was lost. I was in pain and I was hurting. Not just physically, but emotionally as well. I tried my best to deal with 'my new life', but I hated it. I hated who I had become and what I had to deal with. Anyone close to me copped a lot of my anger. I knew I was lashing out and hurting them.

I didn't mean to do it. I saw myself as a thin, ugly, confused and shaken twenty year old who had nowhere to go and no-one to talk to. I often asked God why he gave me the choice to live but he never answered. I felt

so alone.

Despite what everyone told me, I was determined to go back to university. My gap year spent in Germany meant I was already a year older than the majority of people in my year group; I didn't want to fall behind another year. And I knew I would need all the friends I had to get me through the next three and a half years of uni. Plus if I wasn't studying what was I meant to do? Sit at home and feel sorry for myself ? No thank you!

I arranged a meeting with UWA Disabilities Services and Mum and I met with the advisors before uni began. At this point I still struggled to hold a conversation and my voice often faltered. I could barely speak above a whisper. The ladies from Disabilities Services knew it would be hard for me to go back to full-time study after such a traumatic event, but nothing they or anyone could say would deter me from my goal.

I never realised just how much the UWA Disabilities Services did for students until I sat before the represent- atives in a small room just above Guild Village. They explained that there was a room in the library where students could study away from everyone, or lie down for a rest. The ladies said they would write to every single lecturer and the Dean of Arts and the Dean of Commerce informing them of my circumstances.

I was still an outpatient at Fremantle Hospital and had many appointments that I would need to attend on a weekly basis for ongoing voice therapy, physical therapy, endoscopies and ENT clinics. There was a high probability I would need to miss classes throughout the year and so I was able to hand-pick my timetable. That way I could spend the least amount of time at university and walk the least distance between classes.

They also let me coordinate my timetable with Amber. I was so scared of losing marks if I missed class due to hospital. We chose the same units as each other for Communications and Commerce so she would always be able to get my notes and inform the lecturer. The only class we wouldn't have together was German but I had enough friends in that class who could help out.

I was just off crutches when I returned to uni. My ankle hadn't healed accordingly as the break was only discovered three weeks after the accident. It still caused me a lot of pain to walk on, but I didn't want to have it re-broken. I went with Mum to the doctors and was assigned a 12-month ACROD parking sticker that allowed me to park in the disabled bays and drive between classes if need be.

Midway through first semester I turned up to uni as a lady was getting out of a disabled taxi and into a wheelchair. She looked at me in disbelief as I limped away from my car. I felt guilty, because even though I was suffering, at least I wasn't in a wheelchair and I could still use my legs. From that moment on I never parked in a disabled bay again. Instead I would leave for uni an hour earlier and park in the pit.

On the first day back at German class I bumped into a friend.

'Oh my God, are you okay?' she asked. I must have been a

sight for sore eyes. I was deathly pale, had lost over 10 kg in hospital and was wafer thin, like a twig that could snap at any minute. The scars on my neck burned red like fire. They were impossible to miss. Every day I put special oils on them to make them disappear, but they were still as red as ever. I'd only had my stomach tube out for about a week so was thankful at least that wasn't sticking out through my shirt.

The whole first part of the year was a bit of a blur for me. I went between uni and hospital continuously and my attitude to life began to sink lower and lower. My marks also dropped considerably. I slowly started going back to work and I tried a few shifts at the yacht club, but it just wasn't going to work. Although the members meant well, I couldn't serve a drink without being asked how I was. I couldn't handle the constant reminder of my accident, let alone looking directly at the water where I almost died. I sadly resigned and continued with just one part-time job at the accounting firm. I tried my best to balance everything again. Money was going to be tight.

It wasn't easy getting back to 'normal' life. My energy was well below par and my fitness was gone. Mark and I weren't dating anymore but I'd met a nice guy from uni called Tobias, even though I wasn't sure I was ready to date anyone yet. But these things are often out of your control.

I did wonder though whether we could have a normal relationship and if he could he put up with all my injuries. And I wondered if I'd be comfortable enough to eat with him. Amber'd seen me struggle, choke and vomit when eating and knew how embarrassed it made me. And how could I date someone when I had to put my dentures on my bedside table each night? I had to wait another year to have an operation to get teeth because my ENT surgeon didn't want any tubes touching my throat – apparently the nerve endings grow back extremely slowly and he wanted to wait until my throat would be as good as it could get.

And could I forget about Julian who I'd spent so much time with during my exchange in Germany? I still kept in contact and thought about him a lot. What if I'd stayed with him? He had hurt me but he knew me like no-one else. I wondered what he'd think of me if he saw me now. Should I just forget about him altogether? I hoped my diary would provide some answers.

Unsent letters

Dear Julian,

This is not a love letter. I want you to know that because if you expect some soppy account of how life without you is meaningless, then you are in for a lot of disappointment. I'm sorry that my words are sounding so bitter. I wish they wouldn't but today there's probably no way to change my writing approach, let alone to life in general.

I felt a lot of pain when I left Germany and I've blocked it for so long. I need to deal with some things. You know, as soon as I meet a guy who has the potential to distract me from you I panic and run. I don't want to do that anymore. I've met a guy from uni, called Tobias. He speaks German! And I like him so much it freaks me out. He's not perfect. But I like his imperfections. I don't love him.

Not yet to say the least.

I can't fully give my heart away because I'm still holding it in my hand, hoping that one day you will fly out to Australia and claim it. You should never have let me leave on that train. The 12th of January 2007 marks the end of the truest love I've ever felt.

I know religion is a big part of the German culture but I never fully grasped how religious you were. I still don't know. I've never had a religion and still don't but I don't believe you need a religion to believe in God. Now, after my accident, I know for certain there is a God.

I met him.

The place I met him is so hard to describe. The images are still strong. I'll call the place Limbo, even though I'm not entirely sure if it was. I visited Limbo just after my accident, right at the beginning of my induced coma and just after all my life-saving surgeries.

It was a really dark place, shadowed by billowing grey clouds. There wasn't a distinct light source and there were no definite landforms or shapes; everything was dimly lit and grey. The space I was in was clear, yet I wasn't physically there and nor was anyone else. It was as if I didn't have a physical presence; as if my soul or spirit was just a mass of energy occupying a space between those dark grey clouds. I could feel another presence and somehow I knew it was God. We were interacting only by voice and no other physical human aspect existed.

Maybe everyone's meeting with God is different and the interpretation of God when he appears to someone varies depending on a person's beliefs. Maybe to some God is female and to others God could speak Mandarin or have a different ethnicity or maybe even exist in a childlike form. Who knows? I'm sorry if you're not religious. But nor was I.

I wasn't scared. I didn't know where I was, but I knew it was a place I was destined to visit.

God said, 'Kate, you have come to this place because you have a choice to make. You can do one of two things. You can come with me now and this will all be over. Or you can go back.'

I didn't hesitate in replying, 'I'm going back.'

'Kate, you must understand that if you go back it will not be easy. It will be painful. You will have a very long road ahead of you. If you come with me now, it'll all be over. You will never have to experience any more pain again. All you have to do is come with me now.'

'No,' I replied immediately, 'I'm not ready.'

I will never forget that God allowed me to choose my path. I couldn't bear parting this world without saying goodbye to everyone. I also really wanted to see your face one last time.

I could go on for pages but I need to write another letter. I need to write to people because if you trap traumatic things up inside of you then molehills can seem like mountains and it's all downhill from there. The other person I have to write to tonight is Tobias. He's here for me, or at least he really does try to be even though sometimes I know I expect too much from him.

Would you like to know how I met him? You probably don't. I'd better stop writing before I go off on yet another tangent. Ich werde dich bald noch was schreiben. (I'll write you something again soon)

Hab dich lieb Kate xo

Pushing away

Tobias nudged me as I walked past him toward the stairs.

'Na du, wie geht es dir? (Hey you, how you doing?)' he asked with a big, gummy grin plastered across his face. 'Shithouse, hence why I'm going home to bed.' I replied with no sign of emotion, making sure my sunnies remained on my eyes.

'Hey, was ist denn los? (what's wrong?)'

'Everything,' I said with a shrug of the shoulders. 'I'm going home now anyways.'

'Well, where are you parked?'

'At the pit.'

I made my way down the stairs with him hot on my heels. He was wearing his red shirt that I'd seen him wear quite often. He looked really good.

'I'll walk you,' he said as he came shoulder to shoulder with me at the foot of the stairs. 'But you'll have to tell me exactly why you're in this mood. It's such a lovely day!'

'It's a shit day.'

'No the weather I mean, it's beautiful.' He continued trying to lighten the brooding atmosphere I'd built around myself.

'Yeah it is,' I finally agreed, 'But I'm still going home to bed. I don't care how beautiful the day is.'

He studied me with a concerned yet caring look. 'Okay, tell me what's wrong.'

I began to unfold the events of the past few days. First on the list was that things had gone weird between Amber and me. We had a fight over something petty and hadn't spoken since. I missed her. Then Ned flew to America to live for a year. And I had to meet with a lawyer who asked me to write a letter detailing how I mentally and physically 'reacted' to the accident.

Like I really wanted to bring up those emotions again!

I began to cry and Tobias gave me a hug. I was confused by my feelings for him. Really, I thought he was much too nice to get involved with me. I was so complicated. I wanted to be his girlfriend but at the same time I kept pushing him away. I would expect so much of him in the hard times ahead and it just didn't seem fair of me to do that. I told him I had to go and wanted to walk by myself.

I felt like I wasn't normal and never would be again. I felt so angry about everything. I wanted to be invisible; to escape and be free.

Then there was a full article in the paper.

With my parents, I'd been to see a lawyer. I'd been scared as I didn't know what to expect but I knew my life would change course again. I also felt guilty that I had to drag my parents through it and that my dad couldn't retire because of the costs; he'd have to work for five to ten years to cover my medical expenses. I was anxious and wished I didn't have to go down the legal road, but the medical bills were mounting. At my first meeting with the lawyers I was asked to take my teeth out to show I didn't have any. Even though I suspected that was only the beginning of my ordeal, we agreed to issue a writ against Luke and Keith Woollard, suing for damages.

I knew my case against the Woollards might have aroused some interest, but I never expected quite so much. It was the first time my name had been released to the media. My parents had kept it private because they wanted me to recover in peace, but once we'd issued writs that dream was over. It was public knowledge and interest, particularly as Luke's mum, Janet, was a Member of Parliament.

Even though the writs were issued we couldn't actually begin anything until Luke's criminal trial was over. He'd pleaded not guilty to grievous bodily harm and the court kept getting adjourned because of it.

A soul that needs saving

While it was a shame that Tobias and I had stopped seeing each other, at least Amber and I had sorted things out. I was grateful to have her back in my life. The fact that I could call her at midnight bawling my eyes out and hating the world just showed how irreplaceable she was. And I was so lucky to have Mum and Dad. Who could ask for more amazing, supportive parents?

For everyone's sake, I wished I was my old self again. But I was going through a really difficult time and I didn't know how much longer I could cope. Honestly. I played with the idea of just ending it.

The only solution I came up with was to run away. Just pack a bag and take off, escape everything. Nobody would know me, where I came from, what I'd been through or why I was there. But I had too many responsibilities at home and I couldn't just up and leave Mum and Dad. Not at that time. Not to mention my friends or work. But I plotted that the following year, 2009, after my German family had visited Australia, I would try to bail on a semester of uni and disappear.

I prayed to God to make things better and asked him why he threw Tobias at me when he knew it wouldn't amount to anything. Was it to make me realise that there were better things out there than Julian, because if so that was a massive fail. I still couldn't forget Julian.

I needed someone to advise me or help me. My doctor had suggested medication or seeing a psychologist but I wanted someone closer.

Dear Ned

I miss you so goddamn much it's ridiculous. I don't know what to do anymore. I'm so unhappy, but I guess you realised that when we Skyped today. I'm sorry for the way I am. I just can't help it. Life has gotten so incredibly hard, and now that you're not here I don't know where to turn. I also don't want to ruin your exchange year by whining about how shit my life is. That wouldn't be fair on you. I just don't want to be here anymore. I'm sorry I called you with such thoughts, but I'm in such a dark place.

I don't know what I'd do if one of my good friends called me from the other side of the world saying they didn't want to live anymore. I know I have a lot to live for, you don't have to remind me of that … but I just can't anymore, Ned. Thank you so much for taking time to talk to me about it all. I'm sorry to put you in such a hard position. I know there's not much you can do for me while you're in Vermont.

Please come home.

After writing to Ned, I walked around the block. I saw my favourite butterfly, the type I'd always loved as a child because they were nothing like the horrible mothy white ones I used to catch with my net. The beautiful orange and black ones were untouchable. Too fast ever to be caught in a net and I always felt guilty chasing after them. Something so beautiful should never be trapped.

I was nearing the end of my walk when I saw the fluttering in the grass by the road. I stopped to admire it in the passing sunlight and found it strange that it just seemed to flutter in the same spot. I moved closer and realised the butterfly was trapped in a web. I reached down and moved the sticky web away. I didn't think twice about destroying one mystery of nature to save another. Was the butterfly meant to simply die in the web? Too big for a spider to eat and too weak to save itself ? But the butterfly still couldn't get free of the blades of grass. Its wing was caught. I gently worked to free the wing and guided the butterfly up and out of the grass with my hands.

It was hurt, but it could still fly.

Had that been a sign from God? A sign for me to keep going? The butterfly tried and failed. It received help and still couldn't do it. But with a bit of patience and just that little bit of extra help it got there in the end. It flew free. It flew on. Maybe one day I would too?

I wanted to be okay again.

I wanted help to fly again. I couldn't do it on my own.

I thought of a quote by Oscar Wilde: 'Hearts live by being wounded.' It was time to let mine live. I began to look at other positive sayings and writings to remind myself how lucky I was:

A Lesson in Life

Everything happens for a reason. Nothing happens by chance or by means of good or bad luck. Illness, injury, love, lost moments of true greatness and sheer stupidity all occur to test the limits of your soul. Without these small tests, if they be events, illnesses or relationships, life would be like a smoothly paved, straight, flat road to nowhere.

If someone hurts you, betrays you, or breaks your heart, forgive them. For they have helped you learn about trust and the importance of being cautious to who you open your heart to.

If someone loves you, love them back unconditionally, not only because they love you, but because they are teaching you to love and opening your heart and eyes to things you would have never seen or felt without them.

Make every day count. Appreciate every moment and take from it everything that you possibly can, for you may never be able to experience it again.

Talk to people you have never talked to before, and actually listen. Hold your head up because you have every right to.

Tell yourself you are a great individual and believe in yourself, for if you don't believe in yourself, no-one else will believe in you either.

You can make of your life anything you wish. Create your own life and then go out and live it.

-unknown-

A price on my life

Luke Woollard was sentenced on 31 October 2008, pleading guilty to causing grievous bodily harm. District Court Chief Judge Antoinette Kennedy handed him an 18-month suspended jail term and 200 hours of community service. The charge of manslaughter had been downgraded to grievous bodily harm because I had come out of my coma. My life had been publicly valued.

My lawyer called me at work at the accounting firm to ask if I wished to comment to the media about the verdict. I told him I wasn't strong enough to face the media and was too scared to comment. What if it affected my court case?

I hung up the phone and buried my face into my hands and cried. I didn't want to be seen sobbing by my work colleagues so I went into the kitchen, leant against the wall and bit my hand hard.

Jay found me there and led me into the manager's office. By that time I was a blubbering mess. He asked me what had happened and I managed to choke out my hurt. After consoling me, he suggested I take the afternoon off and go home.

I was in a world of shock, sadness and disappointment. I got to my car, locked the door and slumped over the steering wheel.

After a good 20 minutes of wailing, I looked up and saw Janet Woollard, happy and carefree, on a sign promoting her electoral seat of Alfred Cove. I tried to clear my eyes and take some long deep breaths but it was difficult to breathe. I choked as I tried to swallow. I knew I was having an anxiety attack.

Holding on to hope

Anna and Karl-Heinz Benz had been my German parents when I was there on exchange and now they were coming to visit and experience Australia. They were so happy and carefree when they arrived in Perth, but when their kids came two weeks later they began to fuss and make sure they were always doing okay. I don't know why their fussing affected me so much. I had so looked forward to them coming for the festive season and bringing a piece of Germany with them. We toured down south and I snapped at them for no real reason. I felt dreadful and it was out of character. I knew I'd changed and I knew I wasn't the person I used to be. I felt lost. It felt like a piece of me got destroyed in the accident. It was hard to explain, but I think Anna sensed it and she and I sat down and talked about it afterwards. She forgave me but I found it hard to forgive myself.

To get back to my old self, I set some goals for 2009. I wanted them to be achievable and fun, rather than extreme:

- Go back to Germany mid-year
- Run the City to Surf for the first time non-stop
- Go skinny dipping
- Learn to meditate
- Join a dance class
- Party until sunrise
- Learn Spanish
- Listen to one new CD a week
- Volunteer for a community organisation
- See at least one new/up and coming band a month

I needed more than anything to have someone who I could open up to. It seemed most of the guys I'd dated mostly had some link to Germany. Was it because Germany was one of the happiest and trouble-free times? It had to be. It was like I was trying to hold on to the past. I'd been talking to mates in Germany quite a bit in planning my trip and had bought a flexi fare that would enable me to change to an earlier flight as soon as I got my exam timetable.

The year group from my German high school was graduating and there was going to be a big ball in the town hall. As a former class member, I was invited. There were also many other school celebrations planned that I really looked forward to. I also arranged to head to Berlin for five days before the ball to meet up with Ned. I hadn't seen him in almost a year. I missed him so damn much!

Of course the other thing I was excited about was seeing Julian again. We'd been on Skype a bit and he told me he'd written me a million letters but hadn't sent them. I convinced him to post one. I learned that his way of dealing with our separation in 2007 was by going on a drug rampage and hooking up with other girls. He'd wanted to forget me. I tried not to feel bitter. He told me he'd learnt from his mistakes.

I beg you for one last chance, try to forget everything that I've ever done wrong … I will never ever do it again! I promise you that! I want to say so much to you and answer all your questions. That's why I'm so looking forward to you coming to Germany …

Do you know, Kate, on 12 January 2007 I gave up living! Since that day I've felt this emptiness in me, that I haven't really filled and I believe that you feel the exact same. I hope that we can both live an untroubled life again and I will fight until both of us are good again and until we're really truly happy … I still don't know how I'll carry that out, but we will do it. Trust me ☺

There's one more thing I want to say and only then will I stop writing. It's already 1.30 am and I have to wake up at 8 am.

Kate, of course I know that both of us have changed, we've drifted apart, we don't know each other anymore …

I don't know if I love you … which is what you said to me! But I still love the girl I got to know over two years ago and without her life isn't worth living.

Until next time

Deiner Julian

My flight was booked for 13 June 2009 so I guessed I'd find out in a couple of weeks if he really meant it. I still had my end of semester exams to sit but I felt pretty confident I'd pass them all, even Finance which I considered the hardest unit.

The only downside of being in Europe was that I would miss the first attempt at settlement with the Woollards. I'd been to a meeting with Mum and Dad and the lawyers where I signed a contract that gave my parents the right to sit in for me during negotiations. I made it clear to everyone that I didn't wish to accept an offer below $300,000. I'd made a list of real expenses which included:

- Past medical costs
- Future medical costs
- Loss of income and earnings
- Loss of enjoyment of life
- Parents' loss of income and earnings
- Emotional damages

If the Woollards met those expenses it would mean paying for the rest of my operations, reimbursing my parents and I was hopeful that maybe there'd even a little left over to pay some of my HECS debt. And of course there were the legal fees on top of it all. My main hope was that I could finally be free of it all and just be myself again.

An old flame can start a fire

I walked through the exit door of the terminal at Düsseldorf airport. There the girls from my old class were waving an Aussie flag. My other friend Nils stood behind them wearing a sheepish grin and a bright yellow Australian t-shirt that I had given him for his birthday two years ago. Further to the left was Julian. His hair was a lot shorter than it used to be and he seemed a little more stooped over. He was wearing a brown jacket and his piercing blue eyes watched as he nervously stood back.

I rolled my bags down the ramp and stopped as Svea flung herself into my arms. Coco was next in line and I tried my best to mumble some German about how good it was to be there. The last of the girls was Jella. I had to stop my jaw from dropping when I saw her. There was something different about her but I couldn't put my finger on. I soon realised it wasn't the fact that she'd put blonde foils in her hair or the fact that she was a little bit slimmer than last time; she was different because she was grown up, she truly was a w oman.

I then gave Nils a big hug before I looked across to Julian. He held out a long-stemmed white rose and opened his arms. I was overcome with emotion. He smelled just like I remembered. My mouth was dry and I could barely utter a word.

Two and a half years felt like an eternity after every- thing I had been through and I had missed Germany so much. I said goodbye to the boys as my suitcase was chucked in the back of the girls' car. I watched all the signs whizz by on the autobahn and felt a leap of excitement as my hometown's name appeared on a shield. I'd be in Ochtrup in about twenty minutes after driving for almost two hours. The girls suggested a quiet movie that evening at Coco's.

'Klingt gut (sounds good),' I answered in a daze. We arrived at Jella's house and unloaded my bags.

'Give me an hour or two before coming around,' Coco insisted, 'I'll need to clean up a bit!'

Svea headed back to her house and I took my time settling in to Jella's. I said hi to her family and was given my own room upstairs. Memories of my last time in Germany filled me with warmth. Jella asked if I wanted to shower and change before heading to Coco's. I paused thinking that a shower was probably well overdue, but as we were going by bike to Coco's I figured there wasn't much point; we would just be chilling there anyway.

'How about we do a bicycle tour through the town to see what's changed instead?'

'That's a good idea, but we'll need some thick jackets,' said Jella.

I pulled on my jacket and a big warm scarf – even though summer had begun it wasn't exactly warm. We rode through the centre of town and I was surprised to see so many shops had closed down – a telltale sign of the economic times perhaps? I rode past my favourite pizza place and past my old school before getting to Coco's house. I was surprised to see so many people jammed into a small hut in the back of her garden. Her brother must be having a party, I thought.

We parked our bikes along the fence and walked through the garden gate. Coco jumped out of the hut and suggested I say hi to her brother before going inside. I thought it was a bit strange as I'd never had a lot to do with him.

I entered the hut to many wonderful familiar faces. I was completely lost for words. My entire school form group was crammed into the hut for a surprise party. I hadn't seen any of them since my last day of school in 2006. There were about twenty or thirty people, inside and outside, with cartons of beer flowing and heaters cranked.

I was so excited to see everyone; I kind of wished I had showered.

I saw Julian sitting across the table looking at me. I still couldn't bring myself to look him in the eye. The tension between us was intense.

'Let's play floonky ball!' I said.

'Ha ha, really, Kate? You're in Germany less than six hours and already you want to play drinking games?' laughed Simon.

'Not just any drinking game. It's floonky ball! I haven't played this game since last time I was here. It's not legal to drink in the streets in Australia.'

We gathered teams of three and carried a crate of beer onto the side of the road behind Coco's house.

The game involved a plastic bottle and a ball to knock it over and, of course, rules and skolling. I had forgotten about my difficulty in swallowing and could only play two games before it became too hard. Even though they all knew about my accident, I used the cold night air as my excuse to retire from the game.

The night carried on and I was running on no sleep. We had to get more crates from the servo because we ran out pretty quickly. Before I knew it, it was 2 am and the gathering was just beginning to wind down. Everyone began to make their way home.

Only Coco, Jella, Simon, Julian and I were left.

'I need to talk to you,' Julian said.

'I know, but now is not the right time,' I whispered.

'Please, Kate, it has to be tonight.'

I told Jella that Julian and I needed to talk and sort through our issues and asked if it was okay if I went back to his house. She didn't really approve, but she let me go anyway. I knew where the spare key to her house was and I had my mobile on me.

When we were alone in his room, Julian confided that his dad had developed a mental disorder known as narcissistic personality disorder. It meant that he became excessively preoccupied with issues of personal adequacy, power and prestige and pushed anyone close to him away. It had been difficult on Julian.

His puppy had been given away one day while he was at school and his mother and her own sons were eventually kicked out of the house. The father then got a restraining order against them. It wasn't just a threat; the police were called and they had to get their belongings and leave. His mother had taken up two jobs; after being a full-time mother for eighteen years it was a whole new world for her. Julian worked weekends and put a lot of his money towards food and household expenses. He was now the man of the house. Together he and his mum had protected his little brother from the truth and the hurt.

I began to see why Julian never came to Australia when I had my accident, even though it still hurt me. I also understood that he couldn't deal with his life and so he turned to drugs. Not only did he take them, but he dealt them as well. It was his main income. He'd lost a lot of weight. Everybody could see he wasn't well yet nobody had stepped in. He claimed he needed me there to help him clean up, to stop.

I took a step back and let go of his hand.

'Julian, I'm no angel and I'm not a miracle worker. I can't make your problems go away. I have my own problems. Okay, we haven't been there for each other but you didn't even reply to my emails and texts, then you told me you were in love with someone else and then you send me a letter saying I'm the only girl you'll ever love? Bullshit.' I could feel the tears. 'I loved you. I needed you. Where were you?'

'I am so, so sorry, Kate. Please believe me. The biggest mistake I ever made was letting you go. Every day I thought about you. I missed you so much I couldn't stand it. And you weren't here to help me deal with my shit so I blocked my pain with drugs. I didn't know what else to do. You were exactly 17,453 kilometres away from me!'

He came towards me. 'Don't.' I put up a hand to stop him and took a deep breath. 'Just don't.'

He slumped into his computer chair and I stood by the door completely torn. This was the moment when I had to make a choice. He was hurting, but so was I. All I had to do was open his bedroom door and leave and save myself the heartache.

I took a step towards him.

By 5 am we had exhausted ourselves with fears, con- fessions, tears and kisses. We were both emotionally drained. And I needed sleep. We clambered into bed and I rested my head upon his shoulder. We were back together within less than twelve hours of seeing each other.

A much needed break

I caught a train to Berlin to meet Ned. Finally, after all this time, I would see him again. It was a like a day hadn't passed. As soon as we reunited we chatted continuously from the train to the hostel to bars and back on trams. We toured around Berlin by day, saw the sights and learnt about the culture and the history. I introduced Ned to a Berliner Weiße - beer with syrup - which we drank behind the Berliner Dome on deckchairs by the river. I dragged him through the entire city searching for Spaghettieis - ice cream shaped into spaghetti strands, with cream and chocolate sauce. I also bought him a Lebkuchenherz (gingerbread heart) to hang round his neck - a German fun fair tradition. We got to know some people in our hostel and Ned went about romancing some Irish ladies - he hadn't changed a bit! We were the same friends we'd always been and it didn't matter that we'd missed out on a year of each other's lives.

Then I went on to Barcelona to meet Jella. We made the perfect travel pair - she'd get us to where we needed to go and I would get us home again. I liked to joke I was like the dog from Lassie Come Home. Take me somewhere once and I could always find my way back! Being poor students we couldn't afford taxis and decided the metro rail didn't always get us to where we needed to go. We ended up walking everywhere and saw so much of the city. We saw palaces and so many of Gaudi's architectural structures and explored Gaudi's park.

We visited far away towns and one day followed the directions of a nice old man who recommended a particular beach. (I must say Spanish beaches have nothing on Australian beaches.) We'd been walking in 40-degree heat when we discovered he'd led us to a nude beach!

But the Spanish are very open about nudity and the next beach we went to was very similar to the first except that men and women were at least wearing bather bottoms. I asked Jella why women in Europe were so open about exposing their breasts.

She shrugged and said, 'Men don't have to wear a top, why should women?'

I liked that explanation, though I still didn't have the guts to walk around without my bikini on.

Jella and I shared an amazing week in Barcelona and U2 happened to be playing while we were there. We packed a picnic and trekked to the stadium. Sadly we couldn't afford a ticket so we made a quaint little picnic outside on the grass with a guy from the US and a girl from Czech Republic who we'd met on our travels. We bought the food and they bought the sangria. We chilled to the music of U2 and Snow Patrol coming through the stadium roof. It was a great unexpected treat!

Unfortunately when I got back to the hotel that night I made the silly decision to check my emails. There was one from my lawyers who advised that settlement negotiations were going to be harder than first anticipated. I snapped my laptop shut and tried not to let it get to me. I didn't feel like going out after reading that; luckily Jella felt the same.

We arrived back in Germany and Julian picked us up from the airport. I told Julian and Jella about the email from the lawyers. That night I stayed at Julian's and placed his home phone by my bed – just in case Mum and Dad needed to call. They were to stand in for me during the negotiation and I was nervous for them. I was also so grateful to them as, even if I were in Australia, I don't think I would have been emotionally strong enough to attend.

There's no negotiation like a phone negotiation

The phone rang at four in the morning and I sat up in bed, startled. Julian stirred as I answered the phone to Mum's sniffles.

Shit, I thought.

'Hang on a sec, Mum, let me just go downstairs so I don't wake everyone up.' I plodded downstairs and sat in the kitchen. 'Okay so what's happened? I can only expect the worst considering you're calling.'

'Well we went in there and only Keith Woollard and his lawyer were in attendance. The lawyer went on about how you were responsible for getting on the boat and were about 60% liable for doing so,' Mum said.

I was shocked. How was 60% liability even possible if you weren't the driver?

Mum went on. 'They then went ahead and made an offer of $75,000, paid in equal instalments over ten years.'

I swallowed deeply trying to catch the saliva building in my throat. 'Kate, that's all they offered. So we were encouraged to counteroffer, which we did but they didn't accept it.'

I mulled over the situation. 'Okay, so they weren't willing to pay $300,000 so what do we do now?'

'Well no,' Mum said, choking up, 'we counter-offered with $200,000 as advised by our lawyer.'

'You what?'

'Well we had to counter-offer with something and were told $300,000 was too high as they had started so low,' Mum tried to explain.

'But you heard me say no less than $300,000. The lawyers were there and they knew my instructions, too. Thank God the Woollards rejected it, now what?'

'Well after they rejected it they offered $100,000 paid over ten years in equal instalments. I knew you wouldn't accept it so the lawyers have recommended you counter- offer with $150,000.'

'You knew I didn't want to with $200,000 but you did it anyway. Of course I don't want to with $150,000!' I immediately felt guilty.

'We're sorry, Kate, shall we tell them you reject it?' Mum asked, trying to keep her voice steady.

'Yes I reject it,' I said. 'I'm a Finance student and know a dollar today is worth more than a dollar tomorrow. The net present value of that $100,000 would probably only equate to $75,000. I just can't believe this Mum,' I said, breaking down.

'I know sweetheart, it's horrible. Just try and enjoy the rest of your holiday. We're so sorry,' Mum said, crying as well.

'I'm sorry, Mum.'

'I know, Kate. Love you,' Mum replied. 'Love you, too.'

It was just starting to get light outside. I placed the phone on the table and stared at it while trying to breathe. My head started going crazy, the sobs wouldn't stop. I had to get out. I had to move. I had to be anywhere but near that phone.

I wrenched open the front door and it slammed shut behind me. I started to walk and stumble along the street. I couldn't focus as I broke into a jog. I was running from the pain. Trying to escape what I'd just heard.

ORPHAN HOLD
DO NOT SHIP

H1 – 000000000638

ISBN 9780995365506

CLIENT	Alternate Sourcing
STATION	TPP Receiving Station 01
HELD	2026 – 10 – 12 13:40

SHELF

If its order arrives, scan this label at a receiving station.

Going the distance

I returned to Perth with the hope of securing a summer break internship back in Germany, but it would still mean five months before I saw Julian again. I'd also have to work ridiculously hard to earn enough money for another flight and enough spending money to last me three months. I hoped I'd get a good tax refund. I continued working part-time at the tax firm and took up another part-time job behind the bar at Forrestfield Soccer Club.

I was back into the swing of university and catching up with friends. On the first weekend I went to a party and told everyone about my trip. While my close friends weren't surprised I'd got back with Julian, a lot of people didn't even know I had a German boyfriend.

I didn't plan on drinking at the party, but my rubber arm got twisted and I decided to leave my car keys in my bag and stay the night. I ended up crashing in the spare bedroom. In hindsight I wish I had driven.

It was in the early hours of the morning that it happened. At first I couldn't comprehend, but I soon realised what was going on. I screamed the house down, grabbed my things on the way out the door, jumped in my car and drove away in a frenzy of tears. About one in three women will experience sexual assault in their lives. I had become one of the three.

I was extremely upset and confided in Julian. He didn't offer comfort. He said I shouldn't have stayed the night and made me feel extremely guilty.

I began to feel ashamed and blamed myself. I wasn't raped, but I was thoroughly traumatised by what had happened. I was shocked and embarrassed and confided in Amber. She was outraged. I didn't know what to do. I didn't want to go to the police as I was scared of what 'crying assault' would do to my case against the Woollards. Anything could be brought up in court, if it were to get to that stage, and even if criminal charges were pressed, there was no guarantee the charges would go through. It was my word against his.

I did some research and discovered that from the number of women who experienced some form of sexual assault, only one in seven cases were prosecuted. It slowly began to eat away at me as I realised that he would get away with it. Going to university, sitting on committees, and being surrounded by friends kept me going. They distracted me from my pending law case, future operations and the black cloud. I was fighting against depression and, despite recommendations, had refused to take medication up to that point. I wanted to find happiness 'the natural way'.

Eventually, after much convincing by Amber and friends, I stopped being scared and hurt by what had happened. He had taken advantage of me while I slept. It wasn't my fault.

I decided to take justice into my own hands.

I sat down and wrote him an email telling him to stay away from me, my friends and the places I frequented. I told him if he did that, I wouldn't tell anyone what he'd done. If he didn't stay away I would do the following:

- file a police report
- form his parents what he had done to me
- tell all our mutual friends about the incident
- and lastly tell my parents, in particular my Dad.

I finished the email with: 'This is not a threat. You know I am a woman of my word and I will follow through with the above should you not disappear from my life immediately.' Occasionally I saw him around uni, but I would never acknowledge his existence. He was dead to me.

The ultimate decision

I thought of the impending operations and my mood sank lower. The next operation was in early September and my prosthodontist (implant specialist) was in disagreement with my oral and maxillofacial surgeon (jaw surgeon).

My jaw surgeon argued that the best solution for my problem was to take bone from my hip and implant it into my lower jaw, as I didn't have enough bone from where my wisdom teeth had been removed. My prosthondontist, on the other hand, wanted to leave my lower jaw as it was. It would require a lot of bone to hold the implants. He was worried that if the bone didn't take, the operation would be in vain. As the patient, the decision was left to me.

Option 1 – Implant bone from my hip into my lower jaw. Pros:

- My lower jaw would be complete with bone again.
- The bone implant would heal and metal implants would be drilled into the newly implanted hip now-turned jaw bone. Cons:
- I wouldn't be able to weight-bear on my hip for two months (that meant no sport whatsoever and possibly back to a disabled parking sticker to get around uni)
- No exercise for six to twelve months
- The bone might not take
- If the bone did take, it may degenerate over time.

Option 2 – Remove all my remaining bottom teeth except two on either side of my mouth and build a prosthetic bridge.

Pros:

- The prosthetic bridge would fill in the gap in my jaw bone with fake gum and look real despite a gap underneath it.

- The bridge could be maintained for ten to fifteen years before replacement and the bone was not at risk of degenerating.
- No major operation would be needed to replace the bridge.
- I would only need two metal implants on my lower jaw, either side of my mouth, where my teeth once were.

Cons:

- I had already lost nine teeth (two more had to be pulled after the accident through root canal surgery and endodontist recommendations); did I really want to remove nine more?

I tried to remain optimistic, but it was a pretty heavy decision. Uni Games was coming up at the end of September and I had been selected to compete. If I had bone taken from my hip there was no way I could compete. I'd kept quiet about my operations.

I was torn. Anyone I spoke to about it said I should go with option 1. I guess the prospect of losing more teeth scared them. It scared me, too. I used to love my smile. It was mine. It was real. Also, there were many complications involved in a hip transplant, and I loved my exercise. I also didn't know how I'd cope not being able to pound the pavement when I was feeling down.

I eventually chose option 2 for the long-term gain and short-term pain.

Operation # 2

I woke up in hospital but didn't know where I was. I tried to speak. Blood dripped from my mouth and down my chin. My anaesthetist came over and told me to relax. He informed me the operation had gone really well and everything appeared okay.

When I became more aware of my surroundings I realised I was in the post-op ward recovering with other patients. An orderly wheeled me up to my room after some time and I must have looked a sight. My whole chin was bandaged and blood was pooling with my saliva and dripping down my chin and on to my gown. My face was beginning to swell and my head became almost twice its normal size. My lips looked like someone had attacked me with a Botox gun.

Mum and Dad visited that night and left around dinner time. The hospital brought me rice and chicken for dinner and I looked at it in dismay. How was I supposed to eat it? I was so hungry I tried to put rice in my mouth piece by piece, but it kept falling out and getting caught in my stitches. I began to cry from hunger and frustration. A nurse came in to measure my vitals, looked down at my bloodstained food and said, 'Sweet you can't eat that. Tch tch, who gave you that now? Let me go get you something you might be able to eat shall I?'

She took away my tray and returned with a tub of vanilla ice cream. 'Sorry, it's the best I could do with short notice. I'll make sure the right soft meals are ordered for you tomorrow,' she said sympathetically.

I was allowed home three days later and I was spitting into a bag again. The taste of blood was disgusting. My mouth was one giant ulcer and my bottom jaw was a gigantic cut with anywhere between 50 to 100 stitches that lashed around two molars and one lonesome tooth. That remaining tooth would be removed, leaving a hole that the implant could be drilled into during the next operation.

The check-up appointment two weeks later was worse than I expected.

Over the tip of my nose, I watched the doctor examine my mouth.

'Well that's healed really well. You must have stuck to everything we said. Now, let's get those stitches out. There're a few I may keep in as I'm not sure they're ready yet. They're still holding your gums together over the bone and we don't want that coming apart now do we?'

She said what now? I watched a small pair of scissors enter my mouth just under my nose. I heard the clip clip as she began to cut away at the stitching on my top gum.

'Oh this will be so much more comfortable once they're out. Relax your lip, hun. That's it. Yes, you will find it so much easier to eat and to speak. I mean you still can't eat solids but pretty soon you'll be on to bigger better things. Like mashed potato.'

She emphasised the words thinking they would make me happy. Little did she know I'd already tried to eat pasta and rice.

'Nearly done, hun, there's just this tangle of stitches at the back here. From the front I could snip them easily but from the back they're just one big knot.'

The next appointment was at the prosthodontist a couple of weeks later. They tried to fit my bottom denture – which had newly added teeth to replace the ones they had pulled out – when surprise, surprise; it didn't fit. How was my denture meant to fit with my new bone structure?

They took the denture out, drilled the plate to try to fit to the new bone structure and then pushed it back down. I tasted blood and squirmed. They loosely tried the top denture. The whole top palette of my mouth had changed formation from the bone implants and I actually had gum attached to my lip now. Those dentures never stood a chance.

There's another week of uni gone, I thought. I'd already missed the last two weeks as I didn't have any teeth.

There goes work. There goes eating solid food. And there goes the Cott VIP party on Friday night.

The prosthodontist decided to keep my old dentures as a rough guide for making a complete new set. How many 21 years olds could say they'd three different sets of dentures?

Avoiding the darkness

When I was finally allowed back to uni I'd lost a good five kilos from the soft diet. The operation and my three weeks' recovery had provoked the deepest onset of depression yet and it began to spiral out of control. Suicidal thoughts crept into my head and I knew I needed help. I talked to Amber, Ned and Julian about anti-depressants. It was a last resort, but I knew I needed to help myself.

I organised a meeting with my GP who looked up a psychiatrist who would be best suited to me. I was very hesitant, as my past experiences with psychologists had been unhelpful, to say the least. I'd tried three.

The first was directly after the accident and I was forced to see her as a new trauma outpatient. I wasn't coping with not being able to eat or talk properly. But I though her advice was too simplistic. One of her sug- gestions was to not watch television as there were too many food ads to remind me of my situation. I felt like she didn't really connect with me so I stopped seeing her after four or five visits.

The next time I tried a psychologist was at uni. It was towards the end of 2008. I'd gone to Student Services and booked into see an available psychologist. As a UWA student you're permitted to have six free consultations. I didn't tell my parents as I never wanted them to know how much I was struggling. I actually got along with the lady really well and opened up to her about everything.

On my third visit she abruptly told me she couldn't see me anymore, due to my pending court case. It was against UWA policy. I was gobsmacked. I'd spent over two hours baring my soul to this woman. She began to say that she would refer me back to my old psychologist as I grabbed my bag and ran from her office and into the stairwell.

I plonked myself in a corner and sobbed. I try and help myself and this is what I get?

Someone must have told them I was crying at the bottom of the stairwell. A lady from reception came down to comfort me and tried to persuade me back into the office. I refused, lifted my bag on to my shoulder and left. I locked myself in a toilet cubicle near the Guild Village. I missed two tutorials. When I had finally stopped crying I walked with my head down back to my car. I vowed I would never see another psychologist again.

The third was a mental assessment set up by my lawyers to assess how I was after the accident. I was so hostile and angry, not only for being in a room with a psychologist again but also that it would cost me $2000. I could mentally assess myself for free. My diagnosis: I was one messed-up, irrational young woman on the brink of collapse.

Half a year later I was on the brink again. Having been assaulted, having had to make the choice between teeth and walking, my boyfriend being so far away and the black cloud growing. I needed an out. Perhaps a psychiatrist was different to a psychologist. So I bit the bullet.

The psychiatrist was a lovely woman who was very softly spoken. She was astounded that I had never been on medication for depression and anxiety. I told her I viewed it as a weakness. She said something to me I will never forget.

'Kate, it's not a miracle pill. It won't make you better overnight. Think of it like a bandaid; it won't heal the wound, but it will stop the bleeding.'

I liked that. I was bleeding everywhere and the only thing that remotely helped was pounding the pavement. I ran until I was exhausted. I accepted the prescription for anti-depressants and within a month my mood had improved. I felt different somehow, not happy, just not sad all the time.

I went to Uni Games about a month after my operation. I couldn't really play a lot; handball is a contact sport and I was petrified of being hit in the jaw. If I took the court, which was rare, I stayed on the wing too scared to defend attacking players. I tried to look on the bright side: I was on the Gold Coast with my teammates and I was going to make a damn good time of it. If I couldn't play, I'd be the best cheerleader yet!

We played sport by day, hung at the beach in the afternoons and partied by night. We had the time of our lives. As the week wore on, my dentures became looser. The swelling inside my mouth became less and as a result my dentures weren't secure.

On the last night of Uni Games everyone went out to a club to celebrate our silver and we wore the medals proudly around our necks. At the bar, I leaned to yell my order to the bartender. I couldn't talk very loud as my vocal chords were too damaged. As I leaned across, my dentures slipped out of my mouth and on to the bar. The bartender looked down. Horrified, I swept the dentures up, shoved them back into my mouth and kept my hand there to hide my shame.

'What was that?' The bartender asked.

'Sorry, those were my dentures. I have no teeth.'

I immediately pulled away and pushed through the dancefloor and ran out of the club. I was completely mortified. I went home and cried myself to sleep.

The last half of the year continued on and my mood remained stable on anti-depressants. I chatted on Skype a lot to Julian and was accepted into two internship programs: one in Berlin and one in my hometown of Ochtrup. I chose the one with the German tax accounting firm in Ochtrup, to be around friends and family at Christmas time. That way Julian and I could also be close to one another.

I also organised an internship for Julian back in Perth for the month following my return. He would stay six months with my folks and me. Everything was working out perfectly.

Au revoir

'So you've got everything?' Mum asked.

'Yep.' 'You sure?' Dad chimed in. 'It's your last chance.'

'Yes, Dad,' I said, rolling my eyes.

'You know what, Kate. This is the last time

you're going to Germany. I think it's about time people came to visit you for a change,' Dad said with a joking yet semi-serious tone. 'I'm serious, hey. This is the last time.'

I chuckled. 'I'll be sure to tell everyone, Dad.'

I looked at both my parents and my heart swelled. I don't know how to describe that feeling, it could have been pride or joy or love, I think it was a mixture of all three. I was keen to show Julian my life, where I grew up and went to school, where I worked, my university. I wanted him to get to know my friends and family and, really, the whole part of my life that was missing in Germany. The part of me that he never knew but that I wanted him to know. And in three months he would discover it, and fall in love with it. Just like I had fallen in love with Germany.

As I sat on the plane I wasn't as excited as I should have been. The only way to describe it would be to say I felt neutral. I kept telling myself I should be over the moon that I was finally seeing him again. But why did I have to keep telling myself that?

I partly blamed the anti-depressants but the truth was unavoidable. I wanted to stay in Australia and celebrate Christmas with my family and hang with the girls. I wanted to sing, dance and party at all the summer music festivals. I wished to bring in the New Year in a warm climate and celebrate my birthday with friends, barbecuing around the pool. Most off all I wanted to spend Australia Day on the beach listening to the Triple J countdown, chilling with good friends, good food and good vibe. Altogether I was missing the four best days of the summer, and needless to say the year: Christmas, New Year's, Australia Day and my birthday. I was also missing my 'friendship three year anniversary' with Amber. We somehow managed to spoil it every year. Okay, being completely honest, I managed to spoil it every year.

The first year I was just getting out of hospital after my accident. The second year I had just got out of hospital after my first major jaw operation. And now on the third year I wouldn't even be in Australia! I know it's not common to celebrate friendship anniversaries but Amber and I are a little different. It's a private day we wanted to plan where the two of us could be as corny and as girly as we liked.

No, Kate, you're not missing out on anything, I kept telling myself. You're just experiencing something different. Why not try and show everyone in Germany exactly why these days are the best days in the year. Show them why they mean so much to you.

I tried to put a positive spin on things during the long hours on the plane, but the niggle inside my mind was a constant nuisance. I twirled the Saint Raphael pendant my neighbour had given me. It was then I remembered the book I'd shoved into my travel bag. I reached down next to my passport and pulled it out. I let my eyes scroll over the front cover and I saw what Saint Raphael stood for: happy meetings, travel, happy marriage, joy and healing.

Interesting, I thought as I studied the cover. I can understand how everything relates to me, except the happy marriage. I was scared that 'happy marriage' meant Julian would propose and I wasn't ready for that in the slightest. Perhaps instinct was trying to tell me something.

I think my neighbours gave me the book as Saint Raphael is also one of the guardian angels of travellers. But it was as though they knew something else might happen to me while I was travelling, something that I couldn't face alone. I would need a greater power to help me through the German winter ahead and St Raphael would guide me through the hurt and help me to rediscover myself and the world in a new light - not necessarily better, just different.

All I ever wanted

I couldn't contain my wide smile as I saw Julian there watching me. He leaned casually against the wall with a lopsided grin on his face. I dumped my trolley and ran over to him. He scooped me up in his arms and kissed me and my fears were alleviated. My summer was only just beginning, well technically it was winter in Europe but I knew he would be my sunshine and he would keep me warm. I was finally by his side. Nothing could go wrong now, right? I pulled my middle finger at the doubt that had niggled inside of me.

'You dyed your hair!' he exclaimed. 'I knew it!'

'Really?' I asked, genuinely astounded. 'But I kept it a secret and you never saw me on webcam.' 'I know, but I had this sneaking suspicion. Anyway, looks good. How was your flight?' Julian asked, stroking my newly browned hair.

'Aw yeah, the usual. Didn't sleep much so I'm looking forward to a few days' rest before I start work,' I replied. He grabbed my large case with one hand and clasped my hand with the other. We walked through the airport sliding doors and towards the underground car park in Amsterdam; Ochtrup was just over the border. I babbled a lot of tired German. He smiled and listened as I leaned in for kiss after kiss. That's the thing with long distance relationships; you really miss the affection.

Once we were inside the car Julian set the navigation system to home and we hit the autobahn racing. I strug- gled to keep my eyes open and Julian encouraged me to sleep.

'No Julian, the passenger doesn't sleep. It's the rules of the car!' I said.

'Yeah but most passengers haven't flown halfway across the world, Kate.'

I stuttered and had to think about my German; switching from English to German always took a couple of days to get used to. 'True, but I haven't seen you in months. Sleep is overrated. I can sleep when I'm dead.'

He stroked my arm and replied, 'Okay, Schatzi.'

I loved it when he called me that. It is the German version of 'hun' or 'babe' and was always my little German thrill!

Two hours on the autobahn and we'd almost hit home. I loved driving in the car with him. I played with the back of his neck as he drove and his hand rested on my leg or our hands intertwined over the gear stick. We were always touching in some way.

We drove to his Grandma's farm and breakfast was still laid out from that morning. German breakfasts are one of my favourite things in the world. There's normally a big spread of meats and cheeses, with different breads to choose from. Sometimes there'll be hardboiled eggs and fresh tomatoes with freshly boiled tea or coffee to top it all off. Just thinking about it makes my tummy rumble.

But at the time the last thing I was thinking about was my stomach. My eyelids kept drooping and it was so hard holding a conversation with Julian, his aunt and grandma. Trying to stay awake, concentrate and speak German at the same time wasn't working very well for me and eventually Julian bundled me back into the car and off to his house where I finally jumped into bed and nuzzled up to his shoulder.

'Thank you for taking the day off to pick me up,' I whispered. 'I love you.'

'I love you, too. Shh now, get some sleep,' he whispered back.

It was Thursday 10 December 2009. I was safe in the arms of my boyfriend Julian. In two days' time it would be our six-month anniversary. It sounds like a short time to be together but it was a consistent six months that didn't include the time and heartbreak from before. We already knew and loved each other when these six months began so it was different to how most relationships start. The world felt perfect, complete, and I was happy. At least, I thought I was happy.

To celebrate our anniversary that Friday, we had dinner at a Mexican restaurant in the town centre of Bad Bentheim, a town just behind Ochtrup. On top of a hill sat a large castle that was used during war to defend royalty. It was the feature of the town and was a great backdrop to the quaint Mexican restaurant. We linked arms and Julian opened the door of the restaurant.

'After you my lady,' he said.

'Ha! Since when have you been so polite?'

The maître d' came over and ushered us to our table, a small one for two overlooking the courtyard.

'This place would be amazing in summer,' I said. 'I could see a few Sunday sessions going on out in the courtyard!'

'Sunday sessions?'

I choked on my wine a little while trying to swallow and replied, 'Oh yeah, I forget they're a bit of a Perth thing. Basically it's a good excuse to sink a few beverages on a Sunday afternoon with mates at your local or near the beach or some sort of similar setting.'

'But what about work?' he asked.

'It's never stopped us before!' I grinned. 'We'll have to do many sessions when you get to Australia. There is so much I want to show you I don't even know where to begin.'

'Well we've got plenty of time! Now let's order another bottle of wine.'

The evening went smoothly with a lot of banter and reminiscing. He told me about work and I filled him in on uni life. He had just begun his civilian work – compulsory in Germany for male youths once they have finished high school. He opted for that rather than going to the army. He said that he didn't like guns. In hindsight, I think he just didn't want to leave his family.

The demise

I'm not sure when the emotional abuse began. Over the days Julian had made some negative comments but they were so subtle they washed over me. It wasn't until the New Year that I realised things weren't okay. He was very jealous of my guy friends in Australia and it had begun to get the better of him. He believed that when I was back in Australia I had cheated on him.

I was living with him, his mother and his little brother and, though the first few days were a dream to be with Julian, I'd arrived at a difficult time in their lives. Julian's mum's boyfriend moved out as I moved in. I didn't know what had happened between them and felt it wasn't my place to ask. Not even Julian would tell me the reason. It was the elephant in the room. I baked cookies for the family to enjoy but no-one really ate them.

I started my internship on 14 December 2009. I was extremely nervous even though I'd spent the last six months brushing up on my business German. I rocked up in a suit and realised I had overdressed for the occasion. I found out it was okay to wear casual attire to work so long as you weren't meeting clients. I was also relieved that everyone was on an informal level of talk at work. Formal German was like a whole new language to me.

When I arrived home from work Julian had run a warm bath. He'd put scented crystals and candles all around the room. He told me to relax and enjoy myself after a hard day's work. It was really nice. He was always such a romantic like that. He brought up the idea of driving to Paris for New Year. I had four days off over the time and he would have the same days free. We set about planning our trip to the city of love.

Karl-Heinz and Anna invited us to the cinema in my first week of work. I was pretty tired learning to work in a different language, but I wished to make the most of time there and gladly accepted. Avatar had just been released in cinemas and so we went along to a 3D showing a few towns over.

After a week I told Julian that a friend of mine, Ryan, had tried to kiss me. At the time, I told Ryan that I had a boyfriend and of course the kiss didn't go anywhere and we remained friends. My friends in Australia had told me not to tell Julian, they saw it as a non-issue, but Julian wanted to know every little thing and I felt it was the right thing to do. When I told him he was furious. I wondered if I'd explained it incorrectly as Julian thought I'd cheated on him. He made me cut all contact with Ryan. I had to delete his name from my phone and I wasn't allowed to send letters, emails or postcards. It didn't stop there.

Slowly, Julian began to pick fights with me over the littlest things and became extremely controlling and jealous. I'd joined a handball team and he forbade me from attending training. I began to have trouble sleeping. It soon dawned on me that the whole time I'd been there I hadn't seen any of my friends. The anti- depressants I was on made me feel subdued, so I went along with his demands.

One day I came home from work and he had hacked my laptop and got all my passwords for every one of my email accounts and Facebook. He'd looked through my phones – both my Australian and German mobiles and read all the texts in each. He trawled through all my emails and messages looking for signs of something more than a kiss. The sad thing was I thought his behaviour was okay once he admitted to hacking my passwords. He said I wasn't allowed to change my passwords as he wanted to check my account at random just to be sure I wasn't lying. Stupidly, I agreed.

A few days later I got home from work and he screamed at me for changing my email password. I showed him it was still the same.

It didn't matter though. He brought me to tears but then began to comfort me straight after. A pattern was developing and it began to feel like the only time he was happy was when I was upset. He told me I was a different person on anti-depressants and I shouldn't be on them anymore. I agreed and began to wean myself off. He told me things I did around the house weren't good enough, that his exgirlfriends were much prettier than me, that I was too skinny, or I was too selfish. I never felt good enough. Everything I did was wrong.

I thought New Year's in Paris might help things. Getting away from his mum would be a relief and he'd turn back into the man I fell in love with. At 5 am, just as we were leaving, his mother stood blocking the doorway in her dressing gown.

'You're not taking the car,' she said.

I looked from her blazing eyes to Julian. 'Mama, you knew we'd had this trip planned for a while. We've got you Aunty's car for the time being,' he explained.

'You're not taking the car,' she said again. 'Yes we are,' he replied indignantly.

'No! The roads are snowy and it's dangerous. I don't want you driving.'

'Well we're going,' Julian pushed her aside

'Kate,' she grabbed my arm as I went to walk past her after Julian, 'If you leave this house don't ever come back.' She let go of me. 'Both of you don't ever come back again if you leave!'

I was very nervous as I sat in the passenger seat of the car but Julian assured me it was nothing and his mum would be fine when we got back.

On New Year's Eve, without a hotel booked, we left our bags in the car and skirted around town on foot checking out the sights. We saw the Eiffel Tower, cruised the river by boat, and drank Glühwein with waffles. After a lot of searching we finally found a little hotel above a nightclub with one spare single bed – we took it. We went for dinner that night and ate snails and all the traditional French cuisine. We bought a bottle of champagne from the supermarket and walked to the Eiffel Tower to watch it light up ceremoniously in the night sky. It was packed with the people from all over the world, so much so that you could barely move in the street.

We settled on a stone wall and watched the lights change colour and cascade up and down the Eiffel Tower. As the countdown began, everyone counted in their chosen language. At midnight we embraced one another and I felt safe again.

When we got back, his mother was still livid. The tension was mounting and one afternoon when Julian and I went out for a drive I asked him about it. He told me it was my fault and I should get over it and treat her better. I was hurt and demanded he let me out of the car. I walked six kilometres to my host parents' place in Welbergen where I broke down to Anna and Karl-Heinz.

My mood was slipping so I organised to catch up with girlfriends the following weekend. I didn't ask Julian's permission. He acted like he was okay with it but sent me a good eleven texts throughout the night. I'd only gone to dinner and movies with the girls and was home by midnight because Julian and I had planned to go skiing the following day. When I got home there was no sign of him. The clock ticked over 1 am, 2 am, 3 am … still no sign. He finally came home at 5 am. We were meant to be up at 6 am to start the three-hour drive. Stinking of booze, he promised we were still going skiing. I could see it was a lie.

Instead, I went for a big long walk that day. Julian didn't get out of bed until the afternoon. That night I went to a friend's handball game and watched them play. Everyone commented on how terrible I looked. I was fatigued and extremely anxious from everything I was experiencing.

When I got home Julian was sitting stiffly at the kitchen table. Scribbled on a blackboard was a text I'd sent to Ryan weeks ago.

'Get out,' he ordered. 'What?' I asked confused.

'Get out of my house. You cheated on me. You lie to me. I loved you. Get out!' he screamed.

'Julian,' I began, 'Please listen to me. I've told you the entire truth the whole time.'

'I don't need your excuses anymore. You're not who I thought you were,' he said. 'I've called Karl-Heinz, he'll be here to pick you up soon.' I don't remember much else of the conversation. I know I was on my knees trying to wrap my arms around his legs, begging him not to kick me out. His mother and friend watched. As Karl-Heinz arrived and dragged me to the door a hint of the Julian I knew returned. He came up and put his arms around me.

'Shh Mäuschen, everything will be okay,' he said patting my hair.

Karl-Heinz looked at him in disgust and dragged me to the car like a rag doll. I was limp. I was emotionally drained. The person I loved with my entire heart and soul had thrown me out. Thank God for my German family.

When I arrived back at their place in Welbergen, Anna gave me some natural medicine to calm me. She could tell my soul was broken.

'I'm glad you're away from there, Kate,' she said. 'He was destroying you.'

'But I love him,' I whimpered.

'I know, but he wasn't good for you. And as much as I wanted to tell you earlier, you had to experience the horrible to discover it for yourself.'

'How could he throw you out and then hug you as you leave telling you everything will be okay?' interjected Karl-Heinz. 'That's not okay!'

As I slowly calmed down I looked back at all he had done and realised it wasn't right. Karl-Heinz, Anna and I sat and talked until the wee hours of the morning.

Staying strong

I told Julian I would collect my things on the Saturday. Karl-Heinz offered to come with me but I refused. It was something I needed to do by myself. I needed Julian to understand that I was never going back to him. I promised myself I'd stay strong and neutral.

When I arrived he was sitting at the kitchen table and asked me to sit down with him. I refused. He told me to sit and have a coffee. I stood my ground and said I'd rather stand. 'Fine,' he began sullenly. 'Now I know you chose to leave but …'

'I didn't choose to leave, you threw me out.'

'Well now, Kate, you weren't happy with Mama and it was the best solution …' he began.

'Spare me, Julian. I'm not here for a conversation; I'm here to collect my things. You said it, it's over. I won't take long.'

He broke into tears, 'Please, Kate, don't go. Forgive me, I never meant this.'

Instead of buying into it, I went upstairs to pack my suitcase. He spent the time begging me to stay then yelling at me to go; from loving me to hating me. Eventually his mum came and took him away.

I dragged my suitcase down the stairs and into the car. I went back upstairs to do one last look around for the things I had forgotten. I was proud of myself for not crying or giving in to Julian.

Julian told me if I left to never come back.

I put the last of my things in my car before turning to him; 'I'm not leaving, Julian. You threw me out. You ended this, not me. It's over.'

I jumped in the car and drove back to the Benz's. I felt lighthearted and strangely good. I sang along to the radio as my phone went wild with incoming messages. I turned it off.

Over the next few days he sent me a lot of texts, emails and voice messages: apologies, declarations, excuses, reasons, blame, then accusations. I didn't answer any of them. But as the days dragged on and the messages kept coming, I became even more lonely and confused. I missed him. When he sent one last email, something in me shifted:

18 January 2010 Kate,

I love you more than anything.

I'm so incredibly sorry for everything ...

I try to leave you in peace, but I just can't ... this perpetual pull inside of me!

We could just talk, perhaps that'll help.

Can we meet today? The two of us alone? Without anyone else there. Please.

I met him at a restaurant the following day. I talked about the fact that I was doing okay, about how I planned to move out of home when I returned to Australia. The conversation went on for hours. He begged for forgiveness, but I said I could only forgive him with time. As I sat opposite him I realised that even though I was deeply hurt, I still loved him.

He dropped me home a few hours later. As I was leaving, he tried to kiss me. I drew back, holding firm. Then he pulled my head towards his but I struggled and managed to get free. I jumped out of his car and briskly walked up the street away from him, shocked that he'd tried to force me to kiss him. Once I was inside the house I received an SMS: 'Sorry for this message, but I just want to make sure my last words to you are fuck you!' I sat at the kitchen table I stared at my phone in disbelief. I was so confused.

Giving in

I emailed Jay and Amber back in Perth to try and get some perspective and advice. As I talked it through, I realised how many sacrifices I'd made for him. He hadn't supported me and he'd hurt me but he was still under my skin. I could feel a storm brewing and knew I had to be prepared both emotionally and physically. I had to stay strong and love myself.

But sadly all the motivation in the world didn't help and I arranged to meet with him a week later. We agreed to try and make it work, with the proviso that I didn't go to his house the rest of the time I was in Germany. I was still leaving on 12 February 2010 and he was due to come to Australia a few weeks after that and live with my parents and me for six months.

My German friends were so angry with me.

Love can be blinding.

The emotional abuse started again quite quickly. As we were driving one day, he told me that people were judging me. I tried to explain how lonely I felt, but they wouldn't have a bar of it. They couldn't understand why I went back to him.

'Judging me how exactly?'

'Think about it, Kate, it's your second time here this year. Last time you were in Barcelona and Berlin. And even this time you're doing all these different things. Think about how much money that is.'

'Yeah, I know exactly how much money that is, Julian. It comes out of my bank account. I work hard and I save so that I can have fun and spend my money over here and forget about my life in Perth for a while,' I replied, hurt.

'Look, Kate, I'm not attacking you, I'm just defending you against people who don't know these things.' 'Like who?'

'I dunno … people.'

'No, I want to know who exactly. Julian, I worked two different jobs, coached two netball teams, played sport, endured horrible operations, studied full-time and still managed to save my arse off to get here. It wasn't easy but I did it. I lost friends because I never had time to see them and I wouldn't see my family for days on end despite still living at home! And then you tell me I'm shit for wanting to have a little bit of fun here?'

'No it's just that Grandma can't understand how you can spend all this money and do all these different things. Even people in Germany haven't been skiing before,' he said. 'And think about it, you've got this big law case and medical fees to the roof and instead of helping your parents by giving them the money, you spend it on coming to Germany.'

'Oh my God!' I spluttered. 'You didn't just say that. You know nothing about my situation and you never want to hear about it. You always change the subject. Yes, I have medical expenses and, yes, my dad has to work a while longer to secure his once financial future and yes I have spent my own money in coming to Europe. Even if I did offer my dad the measly couple of grand I saved, he would never take it. We're not rich, but we're also not poor. Mum and Dad juggled bills between credit cards and every cent of money earned from their business went to paying those debts off. The medical expenses are over tens of thousands of dollars. My money wouldn't even make a dent in that. We have the lawsuit for a reason. To get that money back. So please tell me again why I should not come to Germany to see my boyfriend? To the place I can escape to and actually be happy in for a while? Is anything good enough for you?'

What Julian didn't realise was that my parents would have paid for my recovery ten times over. They knew that Germany was my escape from the ongoing trauma in Perth. They knew that if we won the legal fight, I would give them every single cent back. I wanted them to have a damn good retirement, because I was the one who had stalled it. He made me sound like I had no appreciation of money or the people around me. It really hurt.

Julian made me feel scared and small, and although his emotional abuse almost destroyed me, he showed me that by pushing me to my limits, I was able to grow into myself again. It was just a process of healing.

Seek and you shall find

It was my German family who helped me find my Kraft. I refuse to use the English word for it because it doesn't have the same meaning, not for me anyway. Roughly translated it means power or strength. It is the thing inside that gives you the ability to go on when you're ready to give up. It forces you to take that extra step. It is the part of you that fights for your life and that helps you stay strong even when you feel like crawling under a rock and staying there.

It was the part of me that I had lost. I had searched everywhere for it but deep down I somehow knew it wasn't there. Since my accident I had never been me, I was a lost wandering soul, a body without a spirit and through a Familliensteller (Family Constellation) I learnt why.

The Familliensteller is probably one of the hardest things in this universe to describe. You need to experi- ence it to believe it. Before I experienced it I would never have believed in something so seemingly ludicrous.

My host mum, Anna, had given me the Familliensteller as a present for Christmas. She had hoped it would help me find myself or deal with my issues. We had a long discussion when she gave it to me and she suggested I focus on an issue for the seminar.

'Anna,' I told her, 'I have so many issues to deal with I wouldn't even know which one to pick!'

She thought for a moment and then said, 'Pick one that surrounds all the negative things in your life. Something that's a key factor in all the problems plaguing you.'

I thought long and hard for a month and with Anna's help I finally came up with what I needed to put forward.

Anna, my host brother Marc, and I woke early on Saturday 30 January to attend a seminar in Altenberger, a cute town about 20 km away. It had been snowing heavily the night before and the roads were quite slippery but we made it on time. The Famillienstellen was held at a small farm deep in the fields. Anna knocked on the door of the farmhouse and asked where the seminar was taking place. The lady grabbed her jacket and wrapped herself up warmly.

She took us round the corner to a barn. It didn't look very cosy from the outside but once inside the warm smell of incense greeted us. The large room only contained a red round staircase, a few chairs, and a table with books. Beyond the table was a glass door that framed white snow against a bright blue sky beyond. It seemed to glitter in the morning sun. I felt the energy of something that scared me. I had no idea what I was in for but I knew it was going to be big.

A few ladies came over and greeted Anna warmly while Marc and I took our shoes off. They took us over to where a square carpet was laid out with about three plastic chairs lined up on all four sides. A few chairs had already been claimed with pillows and rugs.

In the middle of the carpet lay a pot plant with colourful flowers. Surrounding the flowers were five different cards with a picture and a quote beneath. I was curious as soon as I saw the postcard of a sunflower, I had a feeling that card was for me.

Anna had once told me that the sunflower always holds its head high to find the sun. No matter how dark the day, it will always turn toward the light and find its way out of the darkness. Ever since my accident it had become my favourite flower. I, too, wanted to search for the light and hold my head high. So here I was at this Famillienstellen being the best sunflower I could be. Searching for an overall solution to the constant ache in my heart and the emptiness within. The problem I chose to face was 'disappointment'. If you wished to put your problem before the group you had to decide exactly what problem was affecting you most at that time. I didn't know where to begin. It was Anna who said that maybe, just maybe, disappointment would fit every bad situation I have so far experienced.

The biggest disappointment was the accident and the medical and legal difficulties that followed. Another major disappointment revolved around Julian – we had only been back together since the Wednesday of that week and I was still finding it impossibly hard to forgive him. The other major disappointments were to do with my sister, who I'd never really got along with, and my oldest German brother, who I hadn't spoken to since the end of my exchange.

There were about ten of us altogether. Five were there as participants or 'helpers'. The other five were presenting their problem. Each card on the floor had a name on the back. The presenter picked the first card and a lady came up to tell us her problem.

The way it works is that each person puts forward their problem and people around the square are chosen to act out the participant's family. They don't know anything about you, other than your problem, but are put into the energy field to play the participant, the mother, father, brother, grandfather or other person.

The problems put forward and acted out on that day were extremely intense as issues were traced back through the family and solved. Each person took about an hour, making the day very long and draining. But the stories that came out were amazing. No-one knew one other, but once they stepped into the energy field they were exposed to the spirit that was given to them. It seemed, to say the least, crazy.

I had the last card. The sunflower.

I walked up to the lady hosting the seminar, careful not to step on the square of carpet. I told her my problem: disappointment. She asked which family I should put into the energy field first and I wasn't sure. She suggested my German family first and then my immediate Australian family afterwards. I agreed. It was surreal watching people volunteer to play each family member.

The person playing me clutched her throat and said she couldn't breathe. It was like she was being strangled and her throat was caving in. She was trying to breathe, but it hurt. I was shocked. No one in the room knew about my accident except Anna and Marc and they weren't participating. The person who played me wouldn't have known about my accident or my throat which was covered by a huge scarf.

My German family tried to help 'Kate', but she pushed them away. She didn't want anyone close to her. I blinked away tears. After a time the host stopped the role-play and decided my immediate family should go into the energy square. People volunteered to play my mother, father and sister, while the person who played Kate stayed. I placed each person on a different corner of the square to begin with. The person playing Dad went immediately to Kate's side. Mum went over and grabbed my sister's hand and together they walked over to Kate who was still clutching her throat and trying to breathe.

She pushed them away and screamed for them to leave her alone. They wanted to help her but Kate screamed out, 'You can't help me. I've got to help myself!'

The host asked her what she meant. 'I don't know,

I just know no-one can help me,' Kate cried with her hands around her throat.

Tears began to roll down my cheeks. It was like I was seeing myself for the first time.

'How can you help yourself ?' the host asked.

'I don't know,' Kate said. 'There's something missing. I don't feel like myself.'

The host turned to me. 'Is this how you feel?' she asked.

I nodded with tears spilling over. 'Do you know what's missing?' she asked. I shook my head, took a large swallow and whispered, 'Ever since my accident I just haven't felt like myself. I think I died that day, and a part of me died too.'

'So you're missing a part of you,' she repeated thoughtfully. 'How about your Kraft? Do you feel as strong as you used to?'

'No, not at all,' I replied thinking back to how I let Julian bully me and the way I felt when I was on medication.

'Okay, let's put someone in to play your Kraft. I know it's not a physical being, but perhaps that's what's missing,' she suggested.

Someone volunteered. As soon as they stepped onto the rug and into the field they collapsed on the floor and curled up into a little ball. Kate ran over to the Kraft, knelt down and asked where it was. My Kraft began to whimper; it didn't know where it was, it was lost. Kate urged the Kraft to describe the place. My mouth fell open in utter shock. Word for word, my Kraft began to describe the place I had visited once before – the place I called Limbo. My Kraft said it was weak. It couldn't move. It described the God I had seen in Limbo and asked if it could go with him. The Kate kneeling on the floor began to cry and begged the Kraft to come back to her. Someone stepped into the field to play God and with the help of both God and Kate they managed to get my Kraft to its feet. Kate faced God and my Kraft. It was then my Kraft described what had stood behind me on the day of my accident. On that day, if I had turned around and away from God, I would have stared Death straight in the face. Death was there waiting, ready to take me. It was a powerful and frightening realisation.

As my Kraft wobbled on its feet the host told me to step into the square and take my rightful place as the real Kate. I was encouraged to step forward and take my Kraft into my arms, to encourage it to return to me. I hugged the person and cried. I begged, 'Please come back. I need you. I can't do this alone.'

An indescribable warm feeling spread through me. My Kraft hugged me tighter and I felt complete again. Tears flowed down both our faces and once everyone stepped off the rug and on to the side, the whole room was teary. 'Somehow we always save the best for last,' the host said.

My heart was still hurting, but it was no longer empty. My mind felt clearer and I knew the path I'd been taking was wrong.

A rude awakening

Ochtrup was holding a party in the town park on Saturday 6 February 2010 and I thought it'd be a great excuse to celebrate into my 22nd birthday that fell the following day. Before the party, Julian and I had to go to the funeral of his grandmother on his father's side. I could see Julian wanted to go despite not having spoken to his father in years. I told him I would hold his hand the entire time and wouldn't leave his side.

We went along to the evening ceremony and stood at the back. Julian looked at his father from behind and I could see the pain in his eyes. He clenched his fist ever so slightly. I wished I could help. It made me realise that Julian never meant to harm me. Perhaps his mental state had changed just like his father's had, a mental illness that made you cruel to those around you. Those who loved you.

Julian went home after the service and said he'd meet me at the party later. He dished out some harsh words but I wrote it off as a backlash from the funeral and tried my best to ignore his behaviour. I met up with my friends at the Irish pub in town for a beer. At midnight we all celebrated as I turned twenty-two. It was my first birthday in the cold and my first away from home. Julian arrived and came over to my table with a big kiss and a present. He gave me a beautiful silver watch with a round face and round hollow links that climbed from the face and down my wrist like a mismatched ladder. I loved it instantly.

We all walked to the park together and paid the entrance fee for the festival. The tent was the size of a large barn and housed several bars with a raised dance- floor in the middle. There were a few DJs and large speakers all around. Even though it was minus seven degrees outside, it was warm in the tent and everyone left their large winter coats at the cloakroom.

I ran and hit the dancefloor with a few girls. We jumped and twirled around to the German music, singing as loud as we could. One of my favourite songs came on – 'das Fliegerlied' ('The Aeroplane Song'). It's a fun Austrian song that was a huge hit in Germany and has actions that make you pretend to fly, be a strongman, a tiger and a giraffe standing on your tippy toes. Whenever it came on you just couldn't help but dance to it.

My friend grabbed my hand and dragged me to dance on top of some speakers by the DJ booth. I thought about how ridiculous we looked in sight of everyone but had to laugh as the whole dancefloor started joining in the actions and having fun too.

I realised I hadn't seen Julian once since getting to the festival and I went over to the bars to have a look for him. It was pretty packed inside and I had to push past a lot of people. I went from one side of the tent to the other and back again. He was nowhere to be seen. I went back to the dancefloor and one of my friends grabbed me.

'Hey, Kate, did you know Julian was following you the whole time down there?'

'What?' I asked, confused.

'Yeah, while you were looking around, he was just walking behind you at a distance, and whenever you turned around he'd hide behind a pole or a bunch of people.'

'Are you serious? But I was looking for him …' 'Don't worry, he's probably just drunk or something.

Talk to him about it when he sobers up. Come on, let's go find the others and dance some more!' she said.

I reluctantly went with her when all I wanted to do was find Julian and ask why he was acting that way. I did my best to hide my disappointment.

At around 4 am I felt someone grab my arm and I whipped around.

'Julian!' I smiled and threw my arms around his neck. 'Let's dance!'

'No. We're going home,' he said, lowering my arms to my side.

'Now? Can't we stay for a few more songs? I'm not ready to leave yet!'

'I am. Let's go,' he said coldly.

Something was off. He looked ready to pick a fight so I tried a compromise. 'Today's my birthday. I'd like to stay for a few more songs. I'm going in a week and it'll be the last time I can enjoy this kind of thing. If you want to go, that's fine and I can meet you later. But can you stay? Please?'

'No,' he snarled. 'I have your jacket tag and if you don't come with me now you can walk home without it.'

I considered the freezing cold temperature outside. He knew I wouldn't survive a walk to town without a jacket. The dancefloor had started to empty anyway so I figured I may as well go home. I got my jacket and did my final dance through the exit.

That's when the fight began. 'I can't believe you!' Julian said with force.

'For what? Enjoying myself ?' I asked, still dancing to the beats in my head.

'You were dancing like a slut,' he spat. 'What? When?' I asked, taken aback.

'Not once did you get off the dancefloor and then I see you dancing on the speakers. You don't do that!'

'Lots of people do that, Julian. I wasn't the first. Lots of people were already doing it. And it was to 'das Fliegerlied'! It'd take an extra kind of talent to make an aeroplane dance look slutty.'

I shouldn't have made that joke.

'It's not the done thing here!' he shouted. 'You don't do it!'

'Why isn't it the done thing? If I want to dance on top of a speaker I will dance on top of a speaker!' I began to get angry. 'Anyway, how dare you try and control me and tell me what and what not to do. I looked for you all night and my friends say you stalked me while I was looking. What the hell were you thinking? All I wanted was a dance or a birthday kiss. Is that too much to ask?'

'Yes it is!' he screamed. 'You always want too much from me. You're so selfish. How you act reflects on others. I saw you flirting with other guys.'

I glared at him. 'Piss off,' I said angrily. I turned on my heel and started to walk towards the town. I didn't get far.

He grabbed my arm and spun me around to face him. His eyes had clouded over. I didn't recognise him. He grabbed hold of both arms, tightened his grip and shook me like a ragdoll, screaming at me to listen to him. I don't know how long he shook me for, but I was petrified. I froze in fear. When I realised what was happening I began to hit at his chest with my palms to wrench myself free. I twisted and turned but his grip tightened. Then he flung me hard on to the icy, cold ground. I looked up in absolute horror. I didn't recognise the man above me.

In a panic I jumped up and ran. I sprinted through the dark park with tears running down my face and adrenalin in my veins. 'I have to make it to safety,' I thought.

I heard him yelling at me to stop. I ran faster, petrified of what would happen if he caught up. I made it to the centre of town and saw a taxi coming down the street. I jumped in and screamed at the taxi driver to drive. Julian caught up to the taxi and tried to wrench open the door.

'Fahr,' I screamed. The taxi driver floored it and drove me all the way back to my German family's house. I turned off my phone. I shook and sobbed the whole way.

I tipped the taxi driver extra and made my way inside and up to my bedroom where I sat on my bed and rocked for over an hour. Had his emotional abuse really just turned physical? In a couple of hours I would be going to my birthday breakfast with my family.

I stripped off my wet jeans and boots and jumped in the shower letting the water cascade down my face and neck. I towelled off and stood with my face up close to the bathroom mirror. Kate, I told myself, you are a brave girl and you can get through this. You said yourself the storm was rising. You've got to trust your instincts. Try not to blame yourself. In five days you will be on a plane home to Australia. You can do this. Just bluff your way through it.

I took a step back and observed myself in front of the mirror. Bruises were starting to form on my arms from where he had gripped me. I opened my towel and saw my hip had a slight graze, which would also likely bruise and one knee was grazed and slightly red and swollen. All in all I counted myself lucky that the physical damage wasn't that bad and could easily be

I tried to rebook my flights to return home early, but unfortunately they were all full. Anna and Karl- Heinz seemed like they wanted to say 'I told you so,' but thankfully they never did.

When the day of my flight home came, Anna dropped me at the train station. I was petrified of seeing Julian but he was nowhere in sight. As I watched the world pass from the train to Amsterdam, I received a text message.

I want the watch back, it was very expensive and you don't deserve it. hidden by winter clothes. I cursed love and vowed to never talk to him or see him again.

Instinctively I grabbed my wrist. I really liked that watch. Even though it held negative connotations, it was once, for a very short time, a symbol of love. I decided not to reply. That watch would stay on my wrist to remind me to:

- Never give my heart away again
- Trust my instincts, not my heart.
- Never let anyone treat me that way again. Ever!

'Goodbye Julian,' I whispered.

Pulling it together

The day after I returned to Perth, I was to undergo my third operation. I felt broken and the last thing I wanted to do was sit around in hospital with my own thoughts for one to three days. But I also thought the pause might help me to slow down.

The operation was the last procedure needed before I could get teeth fixed into my jaw. Both sides of my bottom jaw would have a tooth removed and a metal rod drilled into it to set for six to eight months. The rod would act as the 'bolt' for the fake bridge that would be put across my mouth.

The top jaw was the worst part of the operation. Now that the implanted bone was considered stable, I would have three rods drilled into the gap where my four teeth were missing. It was decided it would be more aesthetically pleasing if I had a bridge of teeth put across my top jaw, rather than four individual teeth. I had not only lost a lot of bone, but gum as well, so the bridge would allow a fake gum line to be built on top of the teeth.

When I got to hospital I stripped off into the standard blue gown and was wheeled in on a bed to the surgery waiting area. When my turn finally came I was more than ready to go. Following the rules, I hadn't eaten since the night before and food was all I could think about while my stomach did flips.

The white operating room lights shined into my eyes as the nurses put plugs on my chest to monitor my heart rate and jabbed a drip into my arm. I counted backwards from ten. I don't know what number I made it to. I woke up in the recovery area with nurses busily running around caring for post-op patients. I was very groggy and couldn't feel my mouth. I looked down to see the familiar trickle of blood on my gown. I had a bandage wrapped around my head again with ice packs in it.

After a time I was wheeled up to my own room in St John of God hospital. It was late in the afternoon and I was dozing in and out of sleep from all the pain medication. Mum and Dad came to visit and I received a few texts from friends offering encouragement. When visiting hours were over my dinner was brought into the room I looked at in dismay: curry, rice and a bread roll. Not again, I thought.

Mum promised to bring me soft foods the next day. I didn't sleep much that night once I was left on my own. I thought about Julian a lot and my heart ached.

The next day the nurses cleaned away the blood clots in my mouth from the metal rods with small cotton wool buds. I had a few stitches here and there, but definitely not as many as last time. My face was a little swollen, but not too bad. I'd brought in a note pad to write down my thoughts, but I couldn't bring myself to do it. After an assessment by the doctor I begged to be allowed to go home. I was hungry and Mum could take better care of me. I was discharged that afternoon and looked ahead to ten days of soft food again.

February was the peak of summer and I'd be missing out on all the fun stuff at uni. It was O-week and I couldn't even help welcome the new students. Everyone was too busy to come visit. I just sat by the pool and went for walks up to Lesmurdie Falls, mulling over the past and not knowing where the hell the future was going to lead. Now Julian was eliminated from my life completely, I was lost.

The days went really slowly and I began to try and motivate myself to begin 2010 with a fresh start (again). I'd spoken to my mate Nick about sharing a house together. The only thing that held me back before was Julian's arrival but now that he was out of the picture the only thing holding me back was the operation and all my post-op appointments. I organised to move out from my parents' to Mosman Park at the beginning of March.

There were four of us in the house: Nick, his girlfriend, one of his mates and me as the new addition. Nick was the bar manager at Royal Freshwater Bay Yacht Club and organised for me to get a job as a waitress. All four of us worked there part-time during uni. It wasn't long before I received a phone call from a friend asking if I wanted to try for a job at a gym in Cottesloe. I agreed straight away.

I was broke after having lived away with no income so in no time at all I was back to working two part-time jobs while studying. For the first time in my life I was living hand to mouth. Any money I earned went to bills, food and living expenses.

I was quite happy working all weekend and weeknights if need be. I wasn't ready to date anyone and the thought of even touching another person made me feel sick. If I had the time to attend parties I'd always end up D&M-ing in the corner. A group of mates who called themselves the 'Brains Trust' were always there to offer an ear.

Brains consisted of a bunch of law and engineering guys who were extremely intelligent, good-looking and if you spoke to them one-on-one you discovered they had hearts of gold. I always had a laugh whenever I hung with them. They're the kind of guys you'd have as friends for life.

A year of unexpected opportunity

For some reason 2010 was the year when most of my close uni mates moved out of home. Amber moved into a house in Nedlands with three good girlfriends. It was university tradition to name the house that you lived in and so the four girls named theirs The Kitchen.

Ned, who was back in Perth, moved out to Swanbourne with one of his best mates and two other guys from uni. There were four guys in the house so they named it The Lodge like the residence of Australia's Prime Minster. As a house-warming present they received a cement head which they named Kevin Rudd, after the Prime Minister. Kevin became the head of the household - no pun intended.

The Lodge was the party house of 2010. Every weekend friends would gather for Sunday afternoon beer pong and drinks, before strolling to the Claremont hotel for a good old Sunday session. It quickly became a tradition. Over winter The Boys turned their garage into a chill out area with couches and music. They called it The Left Nut. When Julia Gillard became Prime Minister The Boys still let Kevin remain the man of the house but found a red metal heater that they called Julia. Julia chewed through electricity like no tomorrow, pretty ironic given the newly introduced Carbon Tax.

The Lodge made me happy. Ned and I were still the best of mates and I'd spend hours in his room watching documentaries on science and the way the world works. He was writing his thesis and welcomed the breaks. Whenever I couldn't sleep, which was often, I'd go over for midnight Milos - which often consisted of more Milo than milk - and sound advice.

After three months of being back in Australia I was determined to move on. I hadn't spoken to Julian since the night he threw me to the ground, but for some inexplicable reason, I still loved him. I chatted to Ned and Amber for hours on end about it and eventually decided to write him an email. I hated having loose ends and really needed a conclusion to such a long, complicated relationship.

22 May 2010
Hi Julian,

I am going to write this in English as it is my first language. I don't expect a reply. I just want to make sure that you are okay and moving on with your life. We ended very abruptly. I never thought you would touch me like that. I guess you were drunk and jealous.

We came from two different worlds Julian, two different cultures. That created a lot of misunderstanding. Even though it hurts I do believe it is for the best. I love your land and I loved you but I believe that God has something else in mind. I don't know where my future will lead me, but it is already taking me places I never thought I would go. New pathways are opening up and I am beginning to find happiness again.

Despite the mistakes we both made, Julian, I would like to thank you for teaching me to love with every fibre of my being. It is something I will never forget and hope to experience again one day. I hope that you also experience this again.

I'm sorry you never got to visit my world. I think this is what disappointed me the most. I saw many couples moving across the world for each other; from Canada, England and even Norway. And then me to Germany. I just felt like I came between you and your family the whole time. That I was a burden and I never wanted to be that girl. If you would like your watch back I will post it to you.

I pray that you and your family find happiness. That one day you can forgive your father. And that you can forgive me. I pray that one day you can get in touch with the feelings you hide so well. But most of all I pray that you are true to yourself, Julian. Remember that great love and great achievements involve great risk.

I risked my heart for the second time and although it was extremely painful in the end I do not regret being with you. Not at all.

It was around this time that my lawyers decided to pull the writ against Keith Woollard. They felt the case wasn't strong enough and no further negotiations of settlement were happening. During the first semester exam period I received an email from my lawyers. I was at The Lodge with Amber and Ned when I opened the attachment. Keith Woollard had issued me with an invoice of his costs of around $6,000 to defend the writ. Because the writ had been withdrawn, I was responsible for paying the costs. I hadn't been aware of this. It was 10 pm and I walked alone through the streets to Cottesloe beach. I sat out on the groyne and cried.

Once first semester exams were over and I'd applied for special consideration once more, Ned and I decided to book a house on Rottnest for mid-year. The students had organised a dress-up theme and each night they'd walk between houses dressed as pirates or ninjas, getting to know new people and joining in on any household antics. One night in the middle of the week I thought I'd venture out to meet new people.

It was freezing and none of my mates were really keen to leave the warmth so I went off on my own to one of the houses I'd visited before. I had a great time chatting to new people and having some beers; being just an everyday normal girl. I wasn't that girl who had been in an accident, who had an ongoing lawsuit, that girl who'd been sexually assaulted or who was assaulted by her German exboyfriend. At Rottnest I felt like I could be anyone.

I'd forgotten my scarf that night and my tracheotomy scar was noticeably red and pronounced on my throat from the cold. As it was winter my skin was pale, making it even more obvious. If people asked me politely about the scar, I'd reached a point in my life where

I could tell them about it, or if I wasn't in the mood I'd tell them briefly and ask not to talk about it.

Unfortunately that night I had no such opportunity. A guy I'd seen from uni came in. He was friends with some of my friends and had a bit of a reputation as a 'uni turbo'. We'd never really talked before, so I couldn't understand when he turned to look at me and shouted:

'What the hell is Darth Vader doing here?'

I felt the whole room quieten and stare at me as he pointed.

'What do you mean?' someone piped up.

'Look at the hole in her neck!' he shouted and cupped his hands over his mouth and began to breathe like Darth Vader.

I was in shock. Really? Now? Almost three years after the accident.

I ran out the door and along the Geordie Bay road towards the ocean, past a guy I kind of knew. He must have seen my state and chased after me, calling to me to hold up. I blubbered about what had happened and tried to explain why I was so upset. I knew it didn't sound like a lot to an outsider, but that 'hole' had saved my life and sometimes words cut deeper than knives. I'd been offered plastic surgery earlier on in my recovery to have the scar covered or removed, but I had refused. It was a part of me. It had saved my life and I wasn't going to be ashamed of it – at least I tried not to be.

He put his arm around me and told me to ignore all the immature people who knew nothing about life and the shit I'd been through. He was a decent guy and I was thankful to him trying his best to cheer me up. He tucked me into bed that night and said he knew the guy who'd done the Darth Vader act. He gave that guy a right telling off in the morning.

William Tell – eat your heart out

The Rottnest guy, along with some of the Brains crew, was a big influence in getting me involved with the North Cottesloe Surf Life Saving Club. I enrolled to do my bronze medallion in September, just before Uni Games was to commence in Perth. The week I enrolled was the same week I finally got teeth. I still had dentures at that stage. The final procedure was booked for 21 September 2010. I wasn't sure what the dental implant prosthesis would involve; I figured maybe some anaesthesia in a chair and lots of drilling and screwing to get the teeth to fit. I sat in my normal dental chair as my prosthodontist went about inspecting the health of my gums and the metal implants I had put in during February.

He was happy to proceed and began to fit the top- row bridge into my mouth. I felt a bit of pressure on my gums and it was little uncomfortable, but nothing too intense. He then brought out the lower bridge to screw into my bottom jaw. It looked strange, just like those lolly teeth you ate as kid, only hard and with holes to fit the screws. The bottom bridge was screwed into place and a white substance was place over the screw hole to mask the entrance. It was an odd feeling to have a permanent fixture in my mouth.

I ran my tongue along the top row of teeth. I felt the rough of the teeth against the smoothness of the fake gum. The bottom bridge was weirder yet. It had a large metal strip holding it together at the back, which felt smooth and cold. The fake gum line tilted upwards to embed the teeth and there were no gaps between any of my newly set teeth. I was shown how to clean them properly to avoid gum disease and to remove any food that could get caught in the gaps above and below the bridges.

Instead of flossing between my teeth, I had to floss above and below, working on and around the fake gum line. It was ridiculously hard to feed a small piece of dental floss between the small gap at the top of the bridge and my real gum. I had to buy superfloss so the hard plastic thread at the end could feed through holes in tricky places. The bottom gap was a lot larger and easy to feed the floss through. I was given small metal brushes to occasionally scour those gaps. Before I knew it I was on my way.

I wasn't sure I'd get to uni that day and drove towards it in a bit of a blur. I knew I could make my class if I hurried but as I pulled in I thought, What the hell am I doing? I have teeth. I should be celebrating!

I knew exactly what to do. I parked my car and walked to the shops running my tongue along the new teeth. I went through the supermarket doors to the fruit and veg section and up to the aisle of apples. I walked up and down the row first deciding what colour of apple to choose, then what type of apple I wanted and finally, after fifteen good minutes, I chose the biggest, roundest, greenest apple of the bunch. I walked to the counter and proudly purchased my single apple. I wanted to sing and dance and tell the cashier, 'Guess what I'm gonna do with this? I'm gonna bite it, just you watch!'

I walked down the sunny street towards uni rolling the apple in the palm of my hand. This is it, I thought. The day I'd been waiting for, for what had felt like an eternity.

I put the apple to my lips and bit down cautiously. The top bridge pressed ever so slightly into my gums causing a little pressure. My bottom teeth were extremely stable and followed through, tearing a chunk of the juicy apple into my mouth. A trickle of juice ran down my chin and I laughed as I wiped it with the back of my hand.

Ready to invest

Uni Games started a week later and I was excited to be able to play handball properly this time. I was still quite protective of my jaw and teeth, but reminded myself that everything was set in place. I always thought girls had a bit of an advantage on court as guys didn't like to be too rough on girls, whereas I liked to make sure no-one would get through my defence. If it meant I'd end up on the floor then so be it, I'd take the attack down with me. Each night of Uni Games had a theme and the differ- ent teams from universities around Australia would go out partying. Our team decided to rent some dorms at a backpackers in Northbridge where we could go to the bar before hitting the town. There were clubs in Northbridge allocated specifically for Uni Games where students could attend only by showing their passes and IDs.

On the second night, UWA organised a party at a nightclub called the Library for UWA students to have some pizza and catch up on all the sporting triumphs so far. It was at the Library where something unexpected happened; I met someone. His name was Rick. We had both probably had one too many drinks and still to this day I don't quite remember how we met. He was doing sailing and touch rugby; I wondered why I'd never met him before, having known so many people on the touch team. We ended up leaving the club together in the wee hours of the morning and sat outside having a conversation. Well, he mostly did the talking. He told me about troubles that had been plaguing him and it reminded me of my burdens. We walked hand in hand back to my hostel and stopped on every street corner to kiss. We sat outside the backpackers on a bunch of chairs and talked and kissed some more.

I'd lost my phone that night so Rick scribbled his number on my Uni Games tag when we parted. I walked down the hallway to my dorm and couldn't believe I'd been so rowdy as to kiss a stranger! I was turning a new leaf- though I'd broken a team rule: we weren't allowed to kiss others from our university. I hoped no-one would find out.

They did.

I was fined heavily by our team who had monetary fines for stupid things you did on court or out partying. It was all going towards a dinner on the last night. All that day I'd used my teammate's phone to message Rick to confirm our plans for the evening.

I arrived at the club before him and danced around with my team and bumped into some of the touch team. They teased me a little for hooking up with Rick. I told them we were excited about meeting up again and asked if anyone had seen him. His teammate's face dropped.

'Rick's downstairs hooking up with one of the girls from Touch.'

I was determined not to let it affect my night but silently I kicked myself. Stupid.

He's just like the rest of them. Don't invest yourself. Just go out, dance and have fun. He found me on the dancefloor later. 'Hey,' he said.

'Hi.' I brushed his hands off my waist. 'Can I talk to you outside?'

'Sure.' He grabbed my hand and led me out to the balcony.

'Look, your teammate told me you were downstairs hooking up while I was waiting for you.'

His face dropped.

'It's fine,' I said. 'Don't worry about it, that's Uni Games right? You go enjoy it, have fun, but just not with me.'

He was a bit taken aback. 'Seriously, go have fun,' I continued. 'I just don't like to play games. But if that's what you're after I'm sure there are plenty of other girls out there to kiss. Have a good night.' I swept past him, down the stairs, out the door and towards my hostel.

I didn't want him to stop me. I barely knew him, but for someone reason I was really disappointed.

The next morning my teammate came up to me. 'Kate, Rick sent you like ten messages last night to my phone. Saying he screwed up and made a huge mistake. He's begged me to tell you.'

'Don't reply,' I said stubbornly.

I thought about him all day and eventually gave in and messaged him back that evening.

We agreed to meet up at the final UWA party at the Library. I threw my prejudices out the door that night and we greeted each other with a kiss – we were inseparable after that.

When I told Amber about it she found it pretty funny. 'So you're dating a doctor?' she asked.

'Yeah, well he graduates from med this year,' I replied. 'And he's name's Richard?' she asked again.

'Yep, his name's Richard, I confirmed. 'And he's a doctor?' she asked again.

'Yes! Jeez woman how many times do I have to tell you?' I said.

She started laughing, 'Oh my God, Kate, I can't believe you haven't made the connection! You're dating Dr Dick!'

I collapsed in fits of laughter. He wasn't very fond of the nickname.

We had a lot in common – neither of us had done drugs, which was a rarity in our age group, we loved all kinds of sports and enjoyed learning to extend ourselves, even if it didn't fit our intended careers. I soon found out he sailed at one of the yacht clubs I had worked at, South of Perth, and that I actually knew his dad. That's Perth for you!

The romance quickly turned into a relationship. Within two weeks he'd climbed the avocado tree with me, had gone bushwalking and met my family. I soon met his family and before we knew it we'd planned a holiday together. Within three months we were off to Thailand. Rick was the first guy I let all my guards down with and I could be my absolute self. Even around Julian I couldn't do that.

One morning I left Rick sleeping in my bed as I went to do my bronze course at North Cott. I don't know whether the instructors found it funny, or if they simply wished to challenge me but, weighing 58 kg, I was set to rescue a 95 kg guy on a board. That was the day I learnt it was all about technique, not weight or strength.

Afterwards, we all re-grouped on shore and I felt my wrist instinctively. The watch that Julian had given me was gone. I told my instructors and some people in the bronze course snorkelled around to find it. I really loved that watch, but I also wasn't too concerned. I felt like perhaps I was meant to lose it. The ocean, a thing I loved so dearly, had swallowed the one last reminder of Julian. I took it as a sign that I was ready to invest myself in a relationship again.

It's over – you get nothing

In early 2011, I was offered a mid-year graduate position – beginning right after I'd finished my degree. I was stoked. Rick started working full time as a hospital intern and we tried to see each other as much as possible. Ned moved to Sydney to commence his career in finance and I had the feeling life was going to change forever.

It felt like my case had dragged on without movement for about ten months and I tried to contact my lawyers to find out what was going on. I was finally told my lawyer had left the firm. No-one new had been assigned to my case and pre-trial conference was coming up fast. The pre-trial conference is effectively a last-ditch attempt to settle the matter before trial.

The general manager of the Perth office called my parents and me in for a meeting. He said if the pre-trial conference didn't reach a settlement, they didn't wish to proceed to trial and would wipe all fees incurred to date. He was quite sympathetic and said the situation of my case was abnormal, probably because the Woollard's boat hadn't been insured and so there was no insurance company involvement or guarantee of payment even if we won. Four days before pre-trial conference we were assigned a lawyer. I was a little edgy thinking there wasn't a lot of time for her to familiarise herself with the case.

Rick was working on the day and couldn't come to court, but Amber came with my parents and me. We sat in a small room at the district court and waited. My new lawyer and a barrister went across to the Woollard's room to negotiate a settlement. I hoped the woollards would settle, offering me enough funds to cover my expenses.

The door to the room swung open and my appointed barrister entered.

'I'm sorry, it's over, you get nothing,' he said.

I looked down at my hands bunched in a fist on the table. I tried to blink back tears but failed miserably. 'Isn't there anything we can do?' I stammered. 'This can't be the end. We can't have come this far for nothing.'

He placed himself in the seat across the table and looked at me intently. 'They have withdrawn the offer for settlement. The option of $100,000 paid in equal sums over ten years is no longer available.'

Before he left the room he told me there was nothing more he could do for my case. He recommended I didn't go to trial as the defendant didn't have any assets. The best I could hope for was to apply for the criminal injuries compensation claim from the government. Regardless of whether Luke had assets or not, I didn't have $50,000 to fund a trial. I looked out the window at a red brick wall surrounded by wire. I buried my head in my hands. I never knew disappointment could hurt so much.

Mum and Dad hugged me and Amber held my hand. My lawyer said I should tell my story to the media and they would contact their media advisor that afternoon. I didn't know what good that would do for my case, but I did think it would be a good opportunity to raise public awareness on making boat insurance compulsory. It was then I set my mind to it.

Finding my voice

My lawyer's media representative phoned me two days after the pretrial conference. She'd organised an interview with the West Australian and Today Tonight. I had uni that day so I organised to meet with the West at the Matilda Bay tea rooms just across the road from UWA. My parents took some time off work and came along for support.

I sat across from a journalist and talked about my ordeal. It was hard to wrap everything up into one short timeframe, but eventually the interview ended and the journo went home to review the piece and finalise the story. I wandered back across the road to uni, a little bit shaky and with a weird feeling in the pit of my stomach.

I went over to Rick's house in the evening. He was a great support, particularly as he'd only known me for eight months. I was still upset with the result of the pre-trial but tried to look at it positively by setting my new goal. I was going to start fighting for others. I reminded myself that if I could make insurance compulsory on boats then at least some good would come out of this horrible situation.

I guess I misjudged how much the article would affect people.

I woke with a start at 7 am to my phone ringing. 'Hello?' I answered with a gurgle. Mornings weren't the best time for my voice.

'Kate, sorry if I woke you,' said my lawyer's media representative, 'It's just that I've been receiving calls all morning about your article in the West and 720AM would like to do an interview with you.'

'Um okay …' I stammered.

I sat up in bed and took a few deep breaths. What had just happened? No sooner had I swung my legs over the bed, did I receive a phone call from 720AM talkback radio. I would be on their show around 8.30 that morning. I started to gather my things when I received another call. Talkback Radio 6PR wanted an interview as well.

Rick had already left for work and I needed to be with someone for the interview. I couldn't do it alone. I called my parents. I knew they were going on a short holiday that day and hoped I'd catch them before they left. No answer. In a daze, I jumped in my car and tried calling them again; still no answer. I left East Perth and drove down Orrong Road towards their house. 'Please let them just be walking the dog,' I prayed.

Mum called back at 7.30 am just as soon as I hit traffic. I turned into a service station and told her all about my morning and the interviews. I then drove on autopilot towards my parents' house. Everything was in fast forward. I gave my dog a huge hug when I pulled up in the driveway. She was a dope.

All of a sudden my phone rang and the first round of interviews began. I was mindful of what not to say about my case but luckily the focus was on boat insurance. I was so unbelievably nervous. Mum and Dad said I talked really well. I started receiving texts from all over the place. After hearing the interview close friends messaged showing their support. Work colleagues and casual friends messaged in surprise and admiration - they never knew my story and never knew that boat insurance wasn't compulsory in Western Australia.

I'd done quite a lot of research at university on boat insurance in WA and could rattle off a few statistics and facts surrounding the issue to the radio journalists. Most of the callers on talkback were shocked. How could boat insurance not be compulsory? One would assume it's just like a car. That's what I believed until my accident.

Unfortunately the Motor Vehicle Insurance Act of 1943 does not cover boats, even though technically it is a vehicle, with a motor.

My phone rang five minutes after I finished the last radio interview. It was the media representative again. The news channels had been calling and wanted to do a television interview with me. My number was passed on again. I opened my mouth to tell my parents, but my phone rang. It was a journalist from Channel 7. He explained how we would do a 'round' interview so that I didn't have to talk to each channel individually. The interview would be distributed to each station accordingly that day. I agreed to meet him at 11 am at Matilda Bay.

My parents were to leave for the airport at 10.00 am. Mum was sick with worry leaving me in such a media storm, but they had booked their holiday months in advance. I gave Mum and Dad a kiss goodbye, told them not to worry and to enjoy their holiday. Then I called Amber and said I was coming round. She had a one- hour window between my interview and her work shift. As I pulled up outside Amber's house one caller on talkback radio really caught my attention. A girl by the name of Chantelle. Just recently she had also been involved in a boating accident that almost claimed her life. When she listed her injuries I honestly thought she was copying me. I was shocked that someone else had to experience something so awful. I called the station and asked if I could have Chantelle's number, or if they could pass on mine to her.

I was still in my pyjamas and the only clothes I had were the exact same clothes that I'd worn at the interview the day before. I scrounged through my car and found a long green pullover.

'Shit, didn't think about clothes now, did I?' I muttered in annoyance.

I ran into Amber's house in a flurry. 'Amber I need your clothes statt!'

She gave me a hug, 'Sure thing, kiddo, what do you need?'

'Well I've got this weird green pullover thing. Have you got tights, boots and a black singlet? If you do then I have an outfit!' I said without taking a breath. 'Oh and I'll need to borrow some makeup. I don't have enough time to go home and get anything before the interview.'

'Woman calm down!' Amber said. 'We're the same size, we have the same makeup. Go to town.'

I chucked on my clothes and covered any stress pimples with concealer. I ran a straightener through my hair and was good to go in record time.

We set up the interview on a bench by the water. It was the first time in my life I was thankful for studying media and communications as part of my degree. I drew on all that I had learned in class and focused on the interviewer rather than the camera. I tried not to move my head too much or pull funny faces.

I told it like it was.

The camera was focused on my face, but I looked at the Channel 7 journalist while I talked. He showed shock, horror and then sadness. I talked about how I didn't have the $50,000 to go to trial but I wanted to fight for others. To set about bringing justice for future victims.

After the interview, Amber said: 'Kate, that journalist was so taken aback by you. He asked me how you do it. Why you'd want to keep fighting for the boat insurance laws to change, even though it was too late for those laws to help you. He admires you.'

I smiled.

Destiny – meet my doorstep

I woke the next morning at 6 am to a phone call from one of the gym trainers. The gym was meant to be opened at 5.45 am - by me. I panicked and threw on a shirt and pants and ran out the door. I got to the gym in a fluster and apologised to an impatient gathering. They hadn't known who I was and knew nothing about my accident but I noticed some were sympathetic - perhaps they had seen the news the night before?

I scanned everyone through and less than an hour into my shift John Hammond from 6PR turned up. I'd heard him on the radio the previous morning and he spoke very kindly about me and was in support of the law I wished to introduce. I grabbed his keys to scan his tag and my heart started beating.

'John, I just wanted to say thanks for what you said yesterday on the radio,' I said.

He looked at me with confusion, 'What do you mean?' '

Yesterday, on 6PR, you spoke in support of com- pulsory third-party person boat insurance and I just wanted to thank you,' I replied.

He still looked a little bit confused so I continued, 'I wanted to say thank you as I'm the girl from the accident.' His jaw dropped. I couldn't even describe the emotion on his face.

He mumbled a welcome and went in to do his workout. I let out a big breath. John was a powerful man and I'd never had the courage to speak to him before.

An hour or so passed before he came out of the gym and walked straight up to reception.

'Have you dropped your case?' he asked.

No, not yet. We're in the process of doing it now,' I sighed.

'Don't do it. Seriously, don't. I don't have my card on me, but since I've found out who you are, I can't even workout properly. I'll give you my number and you give me a call. We'll organise to meet up and discuss things okay?'

I met with John Hammond on the evening of 23 June 2011. He organised to meet me at the Blue Duck in Cottesloe. I was pretty nervous so I went to the gym beforehand to burn off some extra energy. It was dark by the time I arrived but it was also fairly mild so we sat at a table outside. The sound of the ocean helped calm my nerves. John asked me what I wanted to drink. Caffeine would have kept me up all night and milk always got stuck in my throat. I didn't want to gurgle in front of him.

'I'll just have a mineral water thanks,' I said.

John ordered a bottle to share.

'So Kate, quite a story,' John started.

'Yeah, I can see you were a bit shocked to learn that I was the girl from the accident.'

'I just can't believe I've been going to the gym all the time and never knew.'

'I know,' I replied. 'It's not exactly something I openly talk about.'

'Well what I'm confused about is why you're dropping the case? To me it's pretty open and shut. Why aren't you taking Luke to court?'

'I want to, but my lawyers don't and I don't have $50,000 to fund a trial. Also, Luke says he has no assets.'

John looked thoughtfully at the table. 'So, what about Luke's father? Why didn't you bring an action against him seeing as it was his boat?'

'We did,' I replied. 'We issued a writ the same time we issued one on Luke Woollard. My lawyers later with- drew it, because they said the "duty of care" argument wasn't strong enough.'

'But it was his boat,' said John.

'I know,' I sighed. 'I don't agree they should have pulled it, but it's too late for that now.'

John looked torn. 'You know what, Kate. I have a really large workload at the moment, so I can't personally take on your case. If you were willing to do a lot of the work my firm could maybe take you on. I can't promise anything and I would have to discuss it with the other director first, but perhaps we could take this further.'

I nodded my head because I didn't know what to say.

'I mean, you would have to cover all disbursements and if we needed work done, then we may need your help if the team is working to full capacity,' John continued.

'I've got a lot of mates studying law at UWA. I'm sure if I asked for their help they could help prepare documents and statements.'

'Yes that would be useful,' said John thoughtfully. 'I just know you shouldn't give this up. It's too black and white.'

When my parents returned from holiday, we all met with John. He'd discussed the issue with his firm and advised that Hammond Legal would take me on with certain conditions. One being that John would be unable to take the stand for me in court. He would do his best to find a barrister to work pro bono, but he wouldn't guarantee anything. If he couldn't find one, we would have to be prepared to fork out anything from $10,000 to $30,000. We accepted.

I put a call out to friends and family who might know a barrister who would work upfront. Luckily I didn't have to do much searching as John engaged Glenn Cridland, who agreed to represent me.

Prepping to fight

John approached my former lawyers to obtain my books and records. It would cost me $20,000. I was shocked. John wrote saying, 'Kate Campbell does not have the funds to pay you, which you are fully aware of. Please be reasonable.'

It didn't work. I signed a contract agreeing to pay them $4,500 initially followed up with disbursements until the total amount was paid. Mum wrote out the first cheque for $4,500.

I still remained hopeful that the Woollards would make a serious offer so we didn't have to go to court, but on 29 August 2011, my court date was given out. A two-week trial was scheduled starting on 6 February 2012 – the day before my 24th birthday.

The West Australian contacted me straight away and asked me to do a quick interview with a few photos during my lunch break. I called John to talk to him about it and he said that was okay. The next day I woke up to a text message from a friend.

Front page of the paper! You go girl.

Oh shit, I thought. I got ready for work and drove into the city with Rick. I picked up a paper on the walk to work and was stunned. There on the front page of the West was a full size photo of me. Time for a hair colour disguise, I thought.

I snuck into the accounting firm feeling extremely self-conscious. I had been working there full-time for about a month and hadn't told anyone about my accident or the legal fight. It was such a weird vibe at work that day, no-one said anything. I stuck my head down and focused on my work.

I began to play the waiting game still hoping that somehow the Woollards would settle before it got to trial. I also continued to work on changing legislation to make third-party person boat insurance compulsory. I was ready to make a difference.

I had started lobbying in 2008 when I wrote to the former transport minister, Simon O'Brien. I was told then that boats were a 'recreational hobby' and that 'compulsory insurance for recreational vessels is not a requirement in any Australian jurisdiction, nor are there any plans to introduce such a scheme in any jurisdiction including Western Australia'. On receiving that news I didn't have the energy to take it further. But now that I'd found my Kraft, I was back onto it and I wasn't giving up this time.

I wrote to Troy Buswell as the Minister for Transport and Minister for Housing from the Liberal Party, Ken Travers as Shadow Minister for Transport and Shadow Minister for Finance from the Labor Party, Giz Watson, Member, Standing Committee on Estimates and Financial Operations from the Greens Party and, as an independent MP of Alfred Cove, Janet Woollard, urging them all to consider changing the laws to include a compulsory third-party insurance levy to be built into boat registration fees. Each letter was basically the same and each included some or all of the following points:

- In Western Australia it is not compulsory for boat owners to take out third-party insurance.
- If the boat owner does not insure the boat for third-party damage, victims are required to use the court system if they are to pursue damages.
- Third-party insurance on an average boat ranges from $150 to $450 a year, depending on the boat's value, while a standard car registration includes a compulsory third-party insurance levy of approximately $260.]
- The 'Serious Injuries Due to Water Transport Accidents in Australia' study found that over a three-year period, from July 1999 to June 2003, 2572 people were seriously injured in water transport accidents. This averages 12 new cases per week nationally.

- The National Marine Safety Committee (NMSC) estimated that boating fatalities, serious injuries and incidents cost the Australian community in excess of $370 million each year.
- In Western Australia there are over 94,435 registered recreational vessels and just over 160,293 recreational skipper's ticket (RST) holders.
- Western Australia has an average of five boating- related deaths per year.
- Significant injuries, both fatal and non-fatal, occur on the water. To categorise high-powered boating as a recreational hobby is to turn a blind eye to a serious situation. Introducing legislation will not leave any injured parties in the wake or accident.

I received a reply from Ken Travers' office the very next day and Giz Watson replied within three days. At the time I was moving out of the Mosman Park house to be closer to the city, selling couches on Gumtree and storing other goods, all the while working, but I was keen to keep up the momentum. I met with Ken Travers and chatted about strategies and the best way to keep the ball rolling. I also met with Giz Watson's assistant and then with the Greens MLC, Lynn MacLaren. The meeting with Lynn was in Parliament House on 17 October 2011. While Lynn was keen to introduce a bill immediately, she was advised that the issue wouldn't be able to be looked at coherently until early 2012.

After several meetings with politicians and various email and phone conversations, it was suggested that I write to the Industry and Economics Committee for the Legislative Assembly. I sent an email to the Committee and then wrote to every single MP in Western Australia, addressing compulsory third-party person boat insurance and asking for their support in addressing the Economics and Industry Committee to change current legislation. There were 95 MPs all up. I was yet to hear a response on my initial letter from Janet Woollard and from Troy Buswell who'd also received a couple of my follow-up emails.

Same same but different

I had been communicating with Chantelle from Port Hedland – the nineteen year old girl who'd also been involved in a boating accident and who I first heard speak on 720AM talkback radio. Her tale was heart-wrenching. She had been out on a fishing trip with her boyfriend and his friend. The steering wheel cable on the boat had snapped and flung her across the boat and onto the dashboard. Her facial injuries sounded as severe as mine. Once I tracked her down we became instant friends. The worst part of her situation was that the boat owner had taken out insurance to cover the property only. I couldn't believe that for a mere $150 a year extra, many boat owners opted not to take out insurance for their passengers. Chantelle had been left with no cover for injuries and, unlike me, she did not have the financial support of her parents.

The West found out about Chantelle after I encouraged her to write to her local MP about compulsory third- party person boat insurance. We organised an interview with the media about our push to change legislation and Chantelle flew down to Perth for it. We met officially face to face for the first time. She was gorgeous. I reassured her not to be self-conscious around my family or me as we knew what she had been through and what still lay ahead. The poor thing couldn't even afford dentures and had lived for nine months with no teeth while working to support herself.

We went out for a big family dinner on the first night and talked to Chani about everything she was dealing with. She was young, scared, toothless and in pain. She didn't even have her mum to cuddle – she lived on the other side of Australia. When we got home to my parents' house there were many tears. But there was nothing we could say or do; we knew how horrible it was and there was no guarantee life would get any better. Eventually the tears slowed and she looked forward to the morning when we could begin our joint crusade to change the laws. Like me, it was too late for her; she'd lived through hell but there was no way she was going to let future victims experience the same.

We conducted an interview together by the Bell Tower the next morning and Chani was so brave. I really looked up to her. She spoke openly and honestly to the cameras about her ordeal. She didn't hide her mouth; in fact she showed the whole world that she didn't have teeth. I couldn't have done that at her age. I refused to leave the house whenever I didn't have dentures in. I raced off to work after the interview and Chani flew back home to be with her boyfriend. I was so thankful she had a wonderful guy waiting for her.

Chani gave me even more purpose to keep on with my campaign. After almost two months of waiting and no reply from Troy Buswell's office I'd had enough. I created a Facebook page called 'Make third-party person boat insurance compulsory'. I posted it on my wall and shared it with all my friends urging everyone to write to Troy Buswell, as well as their local MP, asking them to support compulsory boat insurance. Before I knew it, friends began to change their status to request the same thing.

MPs were bombarded with emails and they then wrote to Troy Buswell as 'many people from their electorate had written to them addressing compulsory boat insurance'.

It didn't rest there. Troy Buswell had probably received hundreds of emails regarding the issue, but until I heard back from him I thought it best to keep the pressure on. I began two petitions; one to the Legislative Assembly and one to the Legislative Council in support of compulsory third-party person boat insurance. I emailed the petition to friends and family all around Western Australia. That petition travelled south, through the north and the goldfields, the CBD, the hills and almost everywhere in WA. Chantelle took the petition around Hedland and within a week she had 500 signatures. By two weeks I'd collected 2000. My aim was a minimum of 10,000 so it was only a matter of time before I'd begin door-knocking.

Then, finally, three months after I had sent Troy Buswell the initial letter, I received an email from his office requesting a meeting with me. I was thrilled and scheduled an appointment as soon as possible. Unfortunately, on the day of our appointment fires broke out down south and Troy Buswell needed to travel to the affected area. He'd recently taken on another role as Minister for Emergency Services. My meeting was rescheduled for two weeks later.

Stating the obvious

On 30 November 2011 I spent the day at work in a daze. I held off on my lunch break to use the hour for my meeting. I left work at 2.15 pm to catch the CAT bus up to Parliament House for a meeting at 2.30. I had all my notes bundled up in a notebook and copies for Troy Buswell and his associates to view. I aimed to hit them hard with all the facts.

It was my second time to Parliament House. The first had been to meet Lynn MacLaren, so I was now familiar with having to sign in at the desk and receive a name tag. I was collected by one of Troy Buswell's advisors and was taken to the same room that I had met Lynn in previously. Another man was also sitting in the room and I introduced myself with a handshake.

We conducted some small talk before I delved right into the boat insurance issues. I didn't force my opinion but, rather, stated the facts. Ken Travers and his assistant, Emma, had helped me gather statistics and facts. They were extremely helpful and without their guidance I may not have made it as far as sitting at Parliament House that day.

I referenced the Motor Vehicle Insurance Act of 1943. A simple deletion of the words 'whilst on a road' could make the Act applicable to boats in addition to motor vehicles:

'An Act to require owners of motor vehicles whilst on a road, to be insured against liability in respect of deaths or bodily injuries directly caused by, or by the driving of, such motor vehicles, whether caused on or off a road, to make certain provisions in relation to such insurance and in relation to the awarding of damages in respect of such bodily injuries, and for other purposes.'

I also noted that there were over two and half times more boats on the water now than there were cars on the road in 1943 when the Act was introduced. Boats moored at yacht clubs required compulsory insurance and boats entering Rottnest waters also needed insurance, but nowhere else in WA waters was insurance compulsory.

The component of insurance applicable to people was approximately $150 a year. This small sum could be added to the cost of boat registration or a Skipper's Ticket so that all boats would be covered.

I wasn't leaving out the small boat owners either. Many people who had discussed the issue on radio thought compulsory insurance was unfair. My aim wasn't to punish boat owners, but I believed that if you could afford a boat, you could afford the insurance. I also brought up the most frustrating point of all: the trailer which carries your boat to and from the water is covered by third-party person insurance, but the boat on top of it is not.

Why did people find it more important to insure the property rather than the people on board? Western Australia could take the initiative and put the first foot forward in making the insurance mandatory.

The discussion lasted about thirty minutes. Troy Buswell's closing words stayed with me.

'Kate, you have made some very good points. I'm a boat owner myself and you've got me over the line. I believe this issue needs to be looked into. I think we should engage someone to draft a report to find out what effect this scheme would have on the Western Australian community.'

My mouth almost fell open in shock. I wanted to jump up and dance and hug Troy Buswell but controlled myself as I stood and shook his hand.

The report was finalised at the beginning of June 2012 and was to be reviewed thoroughly by the end of June. It was at this time that Christian Porter left WA Parliament to enter the federal arena. The Treasury position was up for grabs and Troy Buswell made his return as Treasurer. To my delight he kept his position as Transport Minister. But unfortunately, as politics and priorities go, the report was put on the backburner.

The trial begins

The trial began on 6 February 2012, the day before my 24th birthday. There was a huge crowd of reporters on the corner leading up to the court steps. Cameras were focused on me. It was terrifying. I didn't know where to look or what to do. Mum and Dad put me between them and I declined to comment as we made our way up the stairs into court.

Once I was through the doors I realized I had been holding my breath. I let the air escape and went through the metal detectors. We got to the first floor and stood outside the doors of the courtroom. Dad leant over and whispered, 'The Woollards are downstairs in the cafeteria.'

My stomach lurched. I walked slowly over to the glass railing and looked down at the cafeteria. Janet and Luke Woollard sat there and were in a deep discussion with who I guessed to be their lawyers. I stood staring down at them. Wondering.

I was in such a strange frame of mind that day. I felt like it wasn't me there in court. My physical body perhaps, but my headspace was far, far away. I guess it was my way of dealing with it; by not connecting with the situation, I was protecting myself. I was, after all, preparing to take the stand that afternoon.

I remember words from my barrister's long opening speech. 'It's a tale of two worlds colliding and two families colliding,' he said. 'It was the best of times and the worst of times.' The address from the defendant's barrister Raoul Cywicki did not take very long at all. Their defence rested entirely upon whether I knew or should have known that Luke was drunk. If it was deemed I had known Luke was drunk, I would be liable for contributory negligence and any costs awarded to me would be reduced by that amount of negligence.

When my name was called to go on the stand I walked nervously to the front of the room and was asked how I would like to take my oath. I never knew you had the choice of whether you wished to swear on the Bible or not. I'm not religious so I didn't feel it would be right to swear on the Bible. I took my oath and my seat. My barrister, Glenn, first asked me questions about my time in hospital and my recovery process.

I hadn't touched on those memories in years and it was extremely painful. I broke down in tears many times and my voice often wavered. I don't know how long I was questioned for, but I was absolutely exhausted by the end. When Raoul stood up to crossexamine me I was extremely hostile towards him though I didn't mean to be; he was just doing his job. I guess it's a defence mechanism when you're under attack. He had less than half an hour to question me and was cut short to call it a day and begin again the next morning.

I stepped down from the stand exhausted as I hugged my parents and curled up into Rick's arms. The cameras were in my face again as I left court and Rick held my hand as we walked up the street towards his car. I was still shocked by all the media attention. I got home and saw it was one of the top stories on the news that night. I went to the gym to blow off some steam. When I got home I watched a really bad film that wouldn't consume too many brain cells and went to bed relatively early. I'd organised with one of the guys from work to go for an early morning birthday/pre-court jog. We met at our desks before going on a slow river run around the bridges. We chatted a bit about the goings-on but quickly changed the subject to better topics. I needed the distraction.

I worked until I had to be at court at 10 am. Mum and Dad were in the foyer of my building and we walked through the media crowd and into the court together.

I took the stand and was grilled by the defence. Some of the suggestions they put forward made me so angry. I tried my best to maintain my composure but broke down a few times from the harsh questions. They made me feel like I was lying and was in the wrong. At one stage the defence barrister told me to speak louder. 'I can't,' I answered. 'This is as loud as my voice gets.' I was asked to move closer to the microphone.

I was relieved to finally get off the stand around lunch time. When I got outside the courtroom I saw Mum there, bawling her eyes out. The defence lawyers had had her and my father removed as a 'potential witnesses'. My parents weren't even on my witness list. I reassured Mum I was okay and that I hadn't even seen them leave. But inside I fumed; it wasn't fair for my parents.

Amber was due to take the stand that afternoon and came to lunch with my parents and Donna – my mum's friend who came down to be in the room with me in place of Mum. Amber had brought some beautifully iced cupcakes with her. Mark was also due to take the stand that day and he came with his girlfriend and parents. Even though Mark and I had not really seen each other since finishing our German degrees we still held a lot of respect for one another.

Amber went first and did extremely well at the testimonies. I could tell she was nervous, but she had no need to be. She spoke of the events as she remembered them and, not surprisingly, her story was similar to mine. Next on the stand was Mark. I squirmed in my seat as he recalled the night of the accident. He described how he was thrown from the boat into the water. When he climbed back on board he saw me slumped between two chairs. I was choking on my tongue and struggling to breathe. My face was covered in blood and several of my teeth had been knocked out.

'The only [remaining] tooth I remember was through her lip,' he said. 'I hoped she was not conscious.'

Witnessing life through others' eyes

When I got home from court Rick asked what I wanted to do for my birthday. We enjoyed an evening bike ride together as the sun set and Amber had organised movies at her house with the Brains crew so I went around there afterwards. It was a nice evening and I was glad the day was finally over.

The next morning I rode to work early and tried to get as much work done as possible before 10 am. Work never expected me to be there throughout the court process, but keeping my brain ticking over helped distract me from the reality of court. Plus I wanted to make sure my workload didn't go through the roof.

That morning Mark's girlfriend, Kathy, took the stand. She had been the only other girl in the boat that night and the only other person injured – she had fractured her vertebra as she was flipped and flung from the back of the boat to the front.

'I do remember quite clearly Luke being drunk,' she said. 'I remember Luke doing a bit of fishtailing towards the end of the boat ride. I remember yelling at Luke to slow down but that was seconds before the crash so I don't know if there was enough time to react.'

My psychiatrist, Dr Rebecca Adams, took the stand after Kathy. She told the court that the severity of my depression had fluctuated and had been exacerbated by the court process and associated media coverage . She stated that I was one of the most 'determined' patients she had seen in terms of my recovery . She said of my visits : 'She didn 't feel the [Woollard] family acknowledged that she'd been through a terrible experience ... She continued to feel the [Woollard] family response was emotionally , financially and morally inadequate.' 'I get the feeling this case is not just about money,' Judge Philip McCann said.

My parents still weren't allowed in the courtroom and waited outside each day. Rick's aunty came for support the day my psychiatrist and a psychologist gave evidence. She asked if I wished her to leave the courtroom as it was very personal. I asked her to stay, explaining that my life was out in the open for all to see and I had nothing to hide.

On the fourth day of trial my dentist and prostho- dontist took the stand and described my injuries and the ongoing treatment required. We'd never planned to have my parents as witnesses but as they had been removed from court anyway, Glenn decided at least one of them should take the stand. I asked my parents to decide who should do it.

'Like for any parent, it was my worst nightmare,' Mum said.

She broke down but managed to go on.

'We were told we could go and see Kate, but it didn't look like Kate. She looked quite grotesque and not like my Kate at all.'

Mum then detailed my emergency surgeries and the ongoing procedures required to mend my jaw and throat injuries. She told everyone that although it had been more than four years since the accident, and although I had achieved so much, I was still very much affected by my injuries. I still had trouble swallowing, had a quieter voice, and could no longer play sport at a competitive level. Mum also told the court how she and Dad had paid for the extensive medical bills on credit card and using the cash flow from their business.

I noticed one of the water police who had attended the accident and who retrieved the witness statements for the criminal trial sitting in the courtroom. He later told me he'd come to show his support. He was a lovely man and had twice visited me in hospital to get a statement. I remember thinking then that he was very caring. The others on the boat had given their statements within four days of the accident. I wasn't able to give mine until months later, when I could talk again.

At the time of making my original statement, five months after the accident, I was aware of Luke's conviction for his intoxication at 0.119%. When I gave the statement, that knowledge had crept into my recollection, even though that night on the boat I had no idea he was drunk. When an idea has been planted in your mind, you tend to unwittingly lean towards it. This went against me in my crossexamination as two points in my twelve-page statement suggested I knew Luke was drunk at the time: I saw one or two [full] goon bags on the boat, and, I noticed Luke had trouble untying the knot [where the boat was moored] I thought perhaps he could be drunk.

That day in court, however, it was proven that another man, Adam, was meant to be driving that night and that Luke had taken the wheel once I was seated as it was 'his dad's boat'.

Luke took the stand on the fourth day of trial in the afternoon. The West Australian described him as 'emotionless and deliberate in his answers'.

He said, 'by the end of the evening I was a ten out of ten drunk. I would have been slurring words, walking funny, memory gone, just as drunk as you can get before passing out.'

Luke's questioning ran into Friday. He was on the stand much longer than me. His answers didn't stray much from one word: 'Yes', 'No' and 'I don't recall'.

The proceedings finished on Friday afternoon and closing statements were to be heard on Monday. Luke had called no witnesses. I had called nine altogether.

I didn't rest much over the weekend. My mood began to spiral and when Monday came along I had difficulty getting out of bed and heading back to court. The closing arguments from the defence ran for a long time. I felt like my barrister had a lot more to say, but he kept it short so the trial didn't run over to another day. The two-week trial had been cut down to six days, ending on 13 February 2012.

In the closing arguments Judge Philip McCann said there was evidence Luke Woollard had the ability to drive the boat. He stated that Luke had safely manoeuvred his way out of Matilda Bay avoiding up to 50 vessels moored there, headed in the right direction and passed under the Canning Bridge before he slammed into the unlit marker. 'Everything seems hunky dory except for the fact he hit a pole,' Judge McCann said.

Raoul Cywicki suggested Luke was driving on instinct rather than being competent. He argued that – although I had stated in court that I yelled at Luke to slow down – I should have made Luke aware of my concerns by yelling at him or touching him, to alert him to slow down.

Judge McCann rebutted, 'The bottom line is when you get on a boat you sit still and keep your mouth shut'. He asked what more I could have done to get Luke to drive safer, given there was evidence I was holding on tight because the boat was swerving and going fast. The judge said while in hindsight everyone realised the drunken boat trip was 'stupid', there was no evidence that I knew Mr Woollard would drive in such a manner before the boat took off. 'There is no evidence to suggest they were going to do anything other than putt across the river.'

There was to be a three-week wait for the verdict.

Judgement day

At midday on 30 March 2012 I received a call from the West Australian – the outcome of my trial would be announced that afternoon. I called John Hammond's office straight away. They were moments away from calling me and flabbergasted the media had caught on so quickly. John confirmed he would meet me at court for the verdict at 2.30 pm. I had already drafted four responses depending on the outcome.

I met my parents in the lobby of my building and Amber and Rick met us on the corner. Team Brains waltzed in all suited up and John Hammond met us downstairs with Glenn Cridland. Together, we caught the lifts up to the fifth level. Some media were already waiting in the courtroom and I sat nervously between my parents and Rick for the verdict to be announced.

Judge Philip McCann entered and we all stood and bowed. The judgement consisted of 66 pages. Judge McCann summed it up in a few sentences: 'Ms Campbell suffered from some very painful and frankly ghastly experiences as she underwent a lengthy, painful and frustrating rehabilitation process from which there was no relief until the completion of her dental recon- structive surgery.'

The price he put on all my suffering was $229,626.

Judge McCann left the room and I was in shock. I stut-tered to John, 'I don't understand – am I liable in any way?'

John flicked through the court documents quickly with a big smile on his face. 'No Kate, you're not liable. The negligence belongs to Luke. All 100% of it.'

I cried and hugged everyone. I grasped the statement I'd prepared for the media in the event of a positive outcome and left the District Court for the very last time. I shook as I stood on the steps with cameras in my face. My voice wavered as I addressed the media.

'I have prepared a statement. I do not wish to answer any questions just yet. Please direct all questions to John.'

I unfolded the piece of paper and I began to read:

I have found this trial very traumatic and I am very relieved it is over.

It was one thing to endure the endless medical procedures wondering when I would recover, but at least throughout my recovery and the trial I had wonderful people support- ing me, who were always willing to offer their help.

This trial was far harder than I ever expected and I am so happy that it is over and that I will finally get a chance to pay my outstanding medical and legal bills.

It is such a destructive process to have to go through to get justice and I think I will always be angry that the boat wasn't insured, and the way I was forced to fight to get compensation for my injuries.

The defendant clearly spared no expense in defending this action and now that it is over, I sincerely trust that the Woollards will do the right thing, and stand behind Luke, to help my family recover our losses and recover from this awful experience.

I'd like to thank the public and the media who have supported me during this ordeal and I hope you understand that I need some time to let the judgement settle in before I answer all of your questions.

I'd also like to make a special mention of my parents who have always supported me and of John Hammond and his team – I am very lucky to have met John and his team and their generosity and support was so important in my getting my case heard and for justice to finally be served.

I am now very much looking forward to resuming my life without the stress and worry this case has caused my family and I. I can only hope the next chapter will be a much happier one.

The other side

I'd thought it was all over. On Tuesday 24 April 2012 I received an email asking me to phone the West Australian. For the first time, Luke Woollard had released a statement to the media. I was shocked. Why now, almost a month after the verdict? My lawyer was leaving that day for a holiday and would be gone for a month. I realised I'd have no-one to advise me with the media. I was on my own.

I tried not to take Luke's statement personally, but I couldn't help but be unsettled by his hint of bankruptcy: 'My lawyers advise me that an appeal based on Kate Campbell's contributory negligence could well succeed and a wealthy insurance company might well have taken that course of action. However in my case I have limited resources and the only possible outcome is my bankruptcy.'

I was lucky to have my friends' support that day and the next. I tried to take my mind off things with a barbecue and watching the Anzac Day footy clash, but it was all disrupted by intermittent calls from journalists.

That evening Rick came to have dinner at my parents' so we could watch the news together. When I saw him all my stress and frustration unravelled. He planted small kisses on my hair and cheek until I began to calm.

'Thank you,' I said.

'Nichts zu danken (no need for thanks),' he replied.

I smiled and let out a small laugh through the tears. He'd been picking up small bits of German I'd been using around the house when we'd moved in together at the end of last year. It was so cute, as most of the time he didn't have a clue about what he was saying.

We spent the night at my parents' house and I went back to work the next day feeling sombre and brittle. No-one said anything. I guess it was an awkward situation, where no-one wished to touch upon what was happening. I was in the midst of studying. I had enrolled to begin my chartered accountancy in February – just after the trial ended. I figured once the trial was behind me I wouldn't feel so much pressure in my life and would be able to concentrate on both full-time work and studies.

I was wrong.

On Wednesday 2 May 2012 I was nestled into the Reid Library at UWA to commence a day-long study session for my first chartered accountancy exam that I'd be sitting in a week's time. I thought going back to UWA would enable me to knuckle down and study like I used to when I attended uni. Even though I'd graduated from there almost a year ago, I always found it comforting to head back if I ever needed to write or study. The hours I'd spent in that library over the years were priceless. That morning I received texts from a few people asking if I was okay.

I learned that Janet Woollard was on the front cover of the West Australian talking about the accident. My heart sank.

The headline read: 'My Son is not a Monster.'

Oddly enough I never received any calls from the media. I was glad all the focus had been shifted to Janet. I put my head down and tried to concentrate on my books, but the article just kept running through my mind.

At midday I received a text from some of the Brains crew asking if I wanted to grab some Mexican. Those boys always had my back when times were tough. I'd been studying hard and figured a long break might get my mind on the matter again. I met the guys in the car park and we drove to a Mexican takeaway in Subiaco . When I arrived my phone rang. It was an unknown number.

'Hello?' I answered cautiously.

'Hi Kate, it's Channel Nine News,' said a voice on the other end.

The reporter informed me that she'd interviewed Janet Woollard. I couldn't reply with anything other than an 'oh'. Then she told me that she'd asked Janet if I was ever going to get any compensation to which Janet had replied, 'She will never get a cent from my family.'

I hung up, sank down to the curb and put my head between my legs. I wasn't going to cry. I wasn't going to let it get to me. I slowly pulled myself off the sidewalk and made my way back inside the restaurant.

Back at the library in the afternoon I had calls from 6PR and one of the news stations requesting interviews. The news station pushed me hard. I told them I wasn't comfortable being in front of the camera, particularly as I hadn't seen the footage of Janet Woollard. They offered to show it to me and I could do the interview immediately afterwards. I declined. I gave a few lines over the phone and hoped nothing could be taken out of context. At 5.30 pm 6PR phoned back again and, as I was driving, I pulled into the Mount Lawley train station to respond to questions.

That was the second Wednesday in a row where chaos ensued. I hoped it would be the last.

It wasn't.

On Tuesday 8 May I sat my exam. It was worth 70% of my overall mark and I had to pass. I had applied for special consideration with the Institute of Chartered Accountants due to all the media hype. I could feel my anxiety and depression returning so, in a desperate attempt to save my marks, I went to my old psychiatrist to begin anti-depressants again and arrange routine appointments. I couldn't deal with the situation anymore. My application for special consideration was approved and although I fumbled a little in the exam, I hoped I wouldn't need to apply it.

On Wednesday I worked late to catch up on time I'd missed during study leave. I was getting ready to leave around 7 pm, relieved that nothing had transpired for the day, when a strange feeling came over me. Something was out of place, but I wasn't sure what. I googled 'Campbell Woollard' and, lo and behold, discovered that Luke had made a website about me.

Standing tall

The following day I met with Joshua from Hammond Legal, who was standing in for John, and my barrister Glenn Cridland to discuss a means inquiry regarding Luke's claim of bankruptcy. We were still yet to lodge any formal documents, but it was definitely on the agenda. They explained exactly what a means inquiry involved. By law they would be able to look into all of Luke Woollard's assets ranging from bank accounts, material assets right up to trusts. The Act allowed for the plaintiff (me) to call upon anyone supplying a means of support to Luke.

Luke's legal fees had been paid for, which indicated access to a large means of support. We had also discovered there was a Woollard family trust, in which it was more than likely the children were beneficiaries. We agreed that distributions of trust income, trust loans and asset realisations should be explored. I was advised that I could wait up to twelve years before commencing anything against the Woollards – this is how long a judgement debt is allowed to hang in the open.

'Let's proceed with a means inquiry as soon as possible,'

I said. When Wednesday 16 May rolled around I was very edgy but the day passed without incident and I went home that night relieved. But when I turned up at work the next day an email from Hammond Legal informed me that Luke Woollard had lodged a complaint to the Legal Practitioners Board of Western Australia against John Hammond. Luke had claimed that a piece co- written by John Hammond and published in a newspaper was sensationalistic and misleading.

I was upset at first, but I quickly became angry. John had taken me on out of kindness and had given me so much support. I called Hammond Legal and asked if there was anything I could do. John was away on holiday and I felt wretched that his plans of relaxation had been interrupted.

The following Monday 28 May I badly did my knee at our mixed netball semi-final and was off work the next day, my leg raised with ice packs galore. I returned to work on Wednesday with crutches and put my game face on. I knew I probably shouldn't have been at work as I was in pain and wasn't able to weight-bear on my left leg, but it was Wednesday and I was petrified of being at home alone. I received a phone call at midday from Hammond Legal. To my surprise John was back – he'd cancelled the rest of his holiday. He told me that the documents to begin the means enquiry had just been lodged with the court and I should call the media and let them know. I hung up the phone and sighed. I didn't really want to call the media and hoped they'd discover the documents themselves.

No more than ten minutes later I received a phone call from Channel Ten. I couldn't believe the speed of it.

'I'm sure you know why I'm calling,' the reporter said.

'I can guess,' I replied.

'So you've seen the letter?' he asked. 'What letter?'

I asked. 'Oh, I'm calling because Janet Woollard has distributed a letter to all patrons in Alfred Cove addressing her son's court case and claiming you're out to vilify her family,' he stated.

The phone calls didn't stop. Every media source wanted a comment and, as each one called, I informed them the means inquiry documents had been lodged with the court that day. The story exploded. I did radio interviews, print interviews and another round-camera interview. John Hammond was outraged at the letter issued by Janet and immediately wrote a response.

Response to Janet Woollard MP's Letter

Kate Campbell v Luke Woollard

It is entirely inappropriate for Janet Woollard MP to circulate a letter to 20,000 of her Alfred Cove constituents and invite each of them to call her regarding her son Luke Woollard's trial.

A Judge of the District Court has conclusively determined the case.

Luke Woollard did not appeal the decision of the District Court, which found that he was negligent in driving the boat at high speed in a drunken state.

The letter is an attack on Kate Campbell.

The letter suggests that Kate Campbell is dishonest and was motivated by improper reasons in bringing the District Court action. If the reasons for bringing the action were improper, why didn't Luke Woollard raise this with the District Court over the many years that the action was before the Court?

And on what basis does Janet Woollard claim that the District Court action was a strategy designed to 'target the family.' There is absolutely no evidence in support of this outrageous claim.

Janet Woollard states that her family wants closure. Why on earth would you write to 20,000 voters, be interviewed for prime time TV and the printed media alleging Kate Campbell is engaged in a strategy of targeting her family if closure is the desired outcome?

Janet Woollard seeks to dilute the decision of the District Court. That decision found that:

Kate Campbell was an honest person (page 36);

Luke Woollard's statement that he was too drunk to remember what happened was a very damaging admission and [...] may be taken as reliable (page 41);

Kate Campbell did not know that Luke Woollard was as intoxicated as he actually was (page 55);

Kate Campbell did not know Luke well and could not have been well acquainted with his propensity for binge drinking (page 56);

There was insufficient evidence to [...] place Kate on notice that Luke Woollard was too intoxicated to control the boat (page 58);

Kate Campbell's injuries are ongoing – her 14 titanium implants will need to be replaced at 10–15 year intervals. This procedure will be painful [...] (page 64).

Kate Campbell has noticeable scarring (page 64).

Kate Campbell is entitled to 'a very substantial award of damages for pain and suffering, loss of amenities of life, loss of enjoyment of life and bodily and mental harm.' (page 65). $229,000 in damages was awarded in Kate's favour, plus legal costs.

I trust Janet Woollard will ask her 20,000-odd constituents to read every page of the decision of His Honour Judge McCann who listened to the evidence of all parties and their witnesses over 5 days of hearings.

Janet Woollard's letter seriously undermines the importance of the decision of the District Court and unfairly challenges the bona fides of Kate Campbell.

John Hammond

Lawyer for Kate Campbell 30 May 2012

Ready for the next round

Andrew O'Connor from the 7.30 Report had phoned to arrange an interview for that Friday. I was extremely nervous about being on television for a long period of time and could barely keep still at work all day. When I later arrived at ABC headquarters I was whisked away into a small room for makeup and hair before being taken into a studio room with cables everywhere and ushered onto the set.

On the stage were two chairs and a table which I had a bit of trouble getting up to on crutches. I eventually managed to sit behind the table and dropped my crutches at the back of the stage with a thud. I took a deep breath as Andrew quickly ran through what he would be asking. All I managed to say to him was 'Yep. Yep. Uh huh. Yep.'

He began the questions. The interview flowed ridiculously smoothly and was over before I knew it. The manager walked me out, congratulating me on the strong interview. I appreciated receiving encouragement from someone in his profession.

As the following Wednesday approached I braced myself for a storm. What could possibly happen next?

On Wednesday morning I received a phone call from my therapist saying there was a 5 pm appointment available. I took it. Then the Premier of Western Australia made a comment about Janet's letter being unwise. I took it as a positive sign of the day taking a different shape.

At 1 pm I received an email from John. He had been contacted by Luke Woollard's lawyers who wished to have a teleconference at 3 pm. John asked if I would like to join him at his office or whether he should relay the information to me afterwards. I had a gut feeling that I should be there.

I asked permission from my manager and with my walking stick trundled to the bus stop in the pouring rain.

I arrived a few minutes late and John was already discussing things with the lawyers.

'They want to settle,' he whispered with the phone to his ear and his hand over the mouthpiece.

'What?' I mouthed. I wasn't expecting that.

'Let me discuss it with her and I'll call you back,' John said hanging up the phone. 'They've offered $200,000, Kate. I think you should take it.'

'Why?' I asked astounded. 'Why now?'

They didn't give a reason,' John replied, 'But for a moment there things looked pretty dire. It's better than nothing.'

I spoke my thoughts out loud to John.

'Okay, so if I take it, that wipes off my judgement debt, but then all my costs will be deducted from that sum and I'd be lucky to see $40,000. I still don't know what my medical costs are going to be so I'd have to put that amount in the bank to cover future expenses. Basically, I'd get no compensation for loss of earnings, pain and suffering, loss of enjoyment of life, etc.

'… On the other hand, if I don't accept, all offers will be off the table. It could be misconstrued as rejection of a without prejudice offer and then I could lose public support and look greedy even though the amount awarded in court was $230,000 plus costs. I don't want to lose public support. It's what's kept me going.

'… But on the third hand, if there could be a third hand, if I reject it and we do this means inquiry, what if we discover Luke has the funds in the family trust to cover the full amount? I know trusts are generally for tax purposes and the money never really changes hands, but legally he would be bound to those transactions.'

I stayed in John's office discussing the issue for a good hour and a half. I was torn.

He asked if he could counter-offer with $250,000. I thought back to previous settlement negotiations and shuddered.

'Give me 24 hours to think about everything,' I told John.

When I made it back to work there was only fifteen minutes before my therapist appointment at five o'clock. My mind was still spinning at my session and I spent the entire time discussing whether or not to accept the Woollard's offer. I was still conflicted when I finished up an hour later. I hobbled down the stairs to meet Mum and Dad and checked my phone. I had four missed calls from John.

I was worried and called him back immediately. 'Kate,' he answered.

'Hi John, sorry I missed your call. Is something wrong?'

Gob-smacked

It's over!' John Hammond said.

I didn't understand. 'Sorry ... what? What do you mean?'

'They accepted the $250,000 offer. It's over!' John shouted happily.

My heart did a strange flip.

'They ... but ... you ... what ... after so long ...' I wasn't making sense.

'Kate, I have a political contact at the West. I just got off the phone to him. This is front page news tomorrow. They're stopping the papers to run it. Please call him.' John said.

'Okay,' I stuttered searching for a scrap of paper. I jotted down the number and numbly went to meet my parents. I should have been happy, but I was completely in shock. Mum and Dad's car rounded the corner and parked and I got into the back and burst into tears. I couldn't speak.

'Kate what is it?' Mum asked petrified. I continued to bawl but managed to choke out two small words: 'It's over.'

'What, what do you mean "it's over"?' Mum asked. 'J-j-j-jo-John,' I tried.

'Breathe, Kate, just breathe,' Mum said.

'J-J-John counter-offered and they accepted. It's o-over,' I stuttered through breaths.

Mum and Dad didn't know what to say. We all sat in the car on the side of the road crying. 'I've got to tell everyone,' I said. I slowed my breathing and calmed myself before dialling Amber. When she answered she thought the world had ended. I finally managed to get out that it was over and she screamed with joy. Next I called Rick, as soon as he answered I burst into tears again. He said he'd rush home to see me as soon as he finished work.

I called the reporter when I got home but he could barely get a word out of me. I was blubbering and crying so much. I was so happy it was finally over. Everyone I called copped my sobs as soon as they answered. I pretty much drained my phone battery within the first hour. We decided to go back to Mum and Dad's to celebrate with my sister and her husband. I turned off my phone as I knew the media would hit any time after nine that night. We drank champagne and wine and celebrated into the wee hours.

The next morning I overslept. When I turned on my phone I had over twenty voicemails and double the amount of messages. Mum drove me to work as soon as I was dressed and on the way I received calls from 720AM and 6PR to talk about the settlement. I was completely overwhelmed and fumbled with both interviews. I was still in shock. I told others that phoned that we would be holding a media conference at 1 pm that day in John's boardroom.

I arrived at work half an hour late and received congratulations all round. I asked the admin ladies if I could put on a celebratory morning tea but they'd already organised it. Everyone was very supportive and my counselling partner gave a lovely speech. They were surprised to see me at work that day but just because I received a settlement didn't mean life wouldn't continue on.

I left work for the media interview and for the first time I wasn't overwhelmed by the cameras in my face. My sister and parents joined me and my parents overcame their shyness and talked on camera for the first time.

I answered all questions put forward by the journalists and reporters with a strange new sense of calm. I didn't stumble and I didn't fall for any challenging questions or unforeseen curveballs.

A reporter cheekily asked, 'Have you thought about getting into politics with some of those answers?'

'It might be something I consider in the future. I think I've got a thick enough skin for it now!'

Towards the end of the media interview, I gave John a hug for everything he'd done.

'So Kate, what now? What lies ahead?' he asked.

I thought for a moment before replying, 'My life is now a blank canvas, who knows what pictures I'll paint in the future!'

Epilogue

I would have really liked to end this book with, 'and they all lived happily ever after'. One can dream can't they? But, unlike fairy tales, life continues once the story ends.

Not that I wish to end this book on a bad note by telling everyone that 'happily ever afters' don't exist, it's more the fact that I did suffer two more blows once compensation was received. My knee injury turned out to be worse than originally thought and I had to go under the knife for a knee reconstruction as my ACL had been ripped from the bone. So back to hospital it was for me. I tried to remain positive about it all, but was petrified about the painful memories coming back. I guess they'll always be there. I'm still in recovery mode and by the middle of 2013 I was able to start jogging again.

Blow number two came a week after my knee surgery when Rick and I decided to go our own separate ways. I offered him our unit and found a place between the city and the sea. I've missed living close to the beach – it's always been my muse. Rick and I had an amazing two years together and learned a lot from one another. He was my rock when I needed him and I look back on our time together fondly. Perhaps it was just another part of my life that had to end before a new chapter could begin.

The hardest part of this book was not only facing the old demons, but also contacting the ghosts of my past. Each and every person in this book who was not already known by the media gave me their permission to include them. Though, for most people, the names have been changed. Two and a half years after I sent Julian an email telling him goodbye I mustered up the courage to write to him asking whether it was okay to include him in my book and whether there were any parts he wasn't comfortable with that I should change. He answered my email in a way that blew me away. His reply came with the act of forgiveness and finally brought closure:

Wow Kate, I am so impressed. I now understand you more, what you have been through and how the accident has affected you.

Lots of things in this book don't sit well with me – especially our last evening at the tent party ... I remember it differently, but I'm not angry at you for it, or hurt. I'm already okay with everything that's happened and you don't need to change my name. It is our love story told through your eyes, not mine, and I won't stand in the way of that. It's your memories, your book and your healing process.

The best always come last – thank you for letting me read everything before it was published. I know you didn't have to do that and I really do thank you from the bottom of my heart.

I hope we can still have contact every now and again. Take care of yourself

Julian

I'm glad I contacted him and let him read the manuscript. So now quite literally all my loose ends are tied. All old relationships are reconciled, the court case is over, all my bills are paid and what is left over is now sitting in my bank account for any future medical expenses. I will still need to have my teeth replaced every ten to fifteen years, which will be an expensive process. I just hope it's not a painful one. Apart from that my body has healed to 'as good as it gets'. I will never be able to sing or take to the stage as I did in my high school musical, but I remain thankful that I can talk – albeit softly and without much vocal range.

I will always have a swallowing disability, but I'm grateful that I can swallow and have now mastered the art of timing my swallowing when someone else is talking so I don't choke midconversation. It's taken me many years to get over my fear of eating in front of people but now that my story is out, if ever I do cough and splutter over a meal with someone, at least I don't have to explain why. My throat muscles are working to the best of their ability and I actually can't remember what it's like to subconsciously swallow just once.

For me it's normal to gurgle when I talk as my nerves don't pick up the saliva on my vocal chords, to involuntarily cough when saliva goes the wrong way and my nerves don't send signals to my brain telling it to swallow, and to swallow five to ten times for each mouthful of food or beverage I consume. But I'm grateful for the ability to swallow and not having to be fed through a stomach tube for the rest of my life. I have a huge amount of respect for those people who do have permanent PEG tubes.

I'm twenty-five now and there's nothing but a sea of opportunity ahead of me. Who knows where I'll go, what I'll do or who I'll meet along the way. Everything happens for a reason so I must count my blessings. The knee injury provided me with patience to sit down and pin this book together. Without Rick by my side during the last two years I would have really struggled and I hope in the future he'll find someone to make him truly happy. Perhaps my prince charming is out there too but, to be honest, I'm in no rush to find him just yet.

My search for happiness will continue and might be just around the corner. I love the mysteries of life and will keep my eyes open for the right path to follow. At this point in time I can be satisfied that I followed my own 'personal legend'. I know this because I didn't have to sacrifice my moral standing to get where I am now. My experience has taught me that life is full of surprises, but it's also made me believe that without hard times, you can't fully enjoy the good times.

Tell those you care for how much you appreciate them, take each day as it comes and above all, never ever give up on yourself … you never know what the next day could bring.

Until the next chapter …
May peace be with you.

Made in United States
Troutdale, OR
11/06/2025

41411422R00096